BUILD
YOUR OWN
LOG
CABIN

To Jade

oct - 2008

your mum gave me
This book - Long ago

maybe one day you'll
build one -

Love

your Dad
xoxo

BUILD
YOUR OWN
LOG
CABIN

Paul and Karyn Pfarr

Winchester Press

Library of Congress Cataloging in Publication Data
Pfarr, Paul.
   The down to earth no nonsense book on how to build
your own log cabin.

   1. Log cabins—Design and construction.   I. Pfarr,
Karyn, joint author.   II.   Title
TH4840.P43   694'.2   77-17456
ISBN 0-87691-249-8

Book and jacket design by Richard A. Kenerson

Published by Winchester Press
205 East 42nd Street
New York, New York 10017

WINCHESTER is a Trademark of Olin Corporation used by Winchester Press, Inc. under au-
thority and control of the Trademark Proprietor.

Printed in the United States of America

DEDICATION

This book is dedicated to Jimmy Carter, who has been an inspiration to us.

CONTENTS

INTRODUCTION

We wrote this book because our experience convinced us it was needed. When we first went to live in the woods and build our log cabin in Kentucky, we did all the research we could in the available books on the subject. Everything sounded plain and simple, but whenever we actually confronted some problem, we would always find that nobody had mentioned it.

There were plenty of reasons for it. At the time some of the older books were written, many techniques were assumed to be common knowledge, and so were mentioned but not explained. Then, too, we were often too imaginative for our own good. After trying out brilliant ideas no one had suggested, we usually found out *why* they had not been suggested, but by then it was too late. And there was the fact that we were desperately poor. For over a year we had absolutely no cash in hand and no income, and probably none of the books' authors ever imagined that anyone that poor would try building a cabin.

We could understand all these reasons, but it didn't help much. We were still faced with needing a home badly, and not having much know-how to make one.

That cabin was finally finished, and turned out extremely solid and beautiful, but it had taken almost a year and a half to build what should have taken about three months.

For this reason, there is a triple emphasis in this book. First, on extreme detail, to the point of tedium, some may think, but intended to clarify to the point of unmistakability. And we have tried also to discuss what *not* to do, and more important, *why*, for the benefit of other original thinkers.

Second, we have tried to stress those methods that are quick and either very cheap or totally costless, but still durable. People who have plenty of money can always find ways to do things, but for the really poor there are comparatively few ways, and they need to be made clear.

Third, we are especially interested in ease of construction by a single person who has no special strength, or who may even be exceptionally weak.

Many of these methods may be smiled at by those who cannot imagine being forced to use them, but anyone who finds the alternative—living at a city pace—sufficiently unpleasant will be glad they exist, as we were.

One note on ecology: don't let yourself be persuaded that it's immoral to build a log cabin and burn wood for fuel because of the trees cut. Modern houses, too, are often built of timber, which kills trees, not to mention the other materials used, whose production frequently damages the ecology. And all those houses are heated with fossil fuels, which are not renewable and whose production is far more damaging to the ecology. Furthermore, a single day's printing of just one average newspaper, which is thrown away the next day, has killed enough trees to build a hundred log cabins and fuel them for an indefinite length of time. For you to build a home to last for years, and to fuel it with a renewable resource, as the nucleus of a more natural life, is no destruction of the ecology, but a fortification of it.

People are always telling us how you can't just go to the woods, build a cabin, and live in it, in modern times, without a lot of money. This is in spite of the fact that they know we did just that ourselves. You can, too, if you want to. Here's how.

Paul and Karyn Pfarr
October, 1977

1
GETTING STARTED

For us, just starting the cabin project was harder than anything else. A cabin is supposed to be fun to build—and it is, if you proceed calmly, confidently, and with ordinary common sense. But we had very little know-how, and so were not calm or confident. A lack of these mental conditions tends to blow common sense to the winds, too, so that was one strike against us.

Furthermore, having just left the frenetic modern society, we were understandably determined that here, at last, was our chance not to live by the clock. Having too much freedom was another strike against us. Other mistakes we made were equally understandable and equally troublesome. For example, we were camping and could not seem to find time to get meals and attend to camp chores, while still having time to work on the cabin. We were unaware of the necessity for good, sensible working habits, which were part of the very fiber of most of the pioneers, who camped, built, and set up homesteads all at the same time.

Since it's likely that others would also run into trouble with these things, due to the very different pace and life style of the city and the country, we are going to list some of the most valuable principles we learned, not just about working, but about setting up a situation where you get a chance to work on the cabin.

- Keep a schedule. Get up every morning at the same time, and go to bed every night at the same time. Naturally you are not an automaton, but do try to keep your schedule as closely as you possibly can. You may think that you are a creative, imaginative person who stagnates in regimentation, but regularity must be observed if you are serious about getting a cabin built. A schedule will do more to make you feel mentally and physically ready to go than almost any other factor. And don't skimp on sleep; you need more sleep when doing hard physical work than at other times.
- If you are going to be cooking your own meals, particularly over a fire, keep them simple. Plain food tastes good when you work hard, and you

will not be everlastingly bogged down preparing food and doing dishes. If you are camping while you build, don't underestimate the time required for such things as hauling water and getting firewood. You can't just rush off to work in the morning without first seeing that these things are provided for, or you'll be very sorry when the next mealtime rolls around, you're starving, there's no wood cut, and it's starting to pour. Living comes first, the cabin second. Nobody likes this, but it's true.

- Wear clothes you don't have to be careful of and which fit very loosely, so they don't restrict you in any way.

- Work slowly and at a steady pace. A regular pace that you can keep up day after day, good days and bad, will get the cabin done quicker than going fast on your good days and slowly on your bad ones. If you're actually sick, of course, or on the point of getting sick, skip for as long as necessary. Don't try to push through, or you'll probably get worse. But if you're just feeling low, work will often revive you.

- Accommodate yourself to the weather. It is possible to build in the rain (or snow), but efficiency is reduced, and you'll get ahead faster by using such days for tool repair and sharpening, whittling pegs, or perhaps some errand. This is what the old-timers did.

- Don't get sidetracked! You have to do all the necessary living tasks, and have time to relax, but other than that, stick to building. You can't build and have a job, too, not if you expect to get under shelter within a year or two. You may have plans to paint, or raise domestic animals, or garden, or write books, later, but you aren't doing that now. You are building. Even the settlers did not usually garden when their cabins were in progress, although they were undoubtedly more proficient at both cabin-building and gardening than most of us are today. A cabin is a big project, and takes patient, single-minded work every day if it is to get done.

- Don't let yourself be disappointed if progress is slower than you expected. It frequently is, even under ideal conditions, which few of us have. Just set your sights on doing at least one thing on the project every day, and it will soon be done. If we had managed to lay just one log a day, our first cabin would have been done much more quickly than it was. And always, when the walls get above 3 feet, you will find that you gain enthusiasm.

The typical pioneer, unlike most modern people, had been taught all these things when he was a child. He and his family would drive their covered wagon to an ideal site, get out, unload the wagon, take the wagon box off the running gear, and off he'd go to get a load of logs. It sounds wonderfully simple but, unfortunately, circumstances today are usually considerably more complicated.

Take that ideal site, for instance. The pioneer was homesteading in new, unsettled territory. He could pick a convenient location where all the things he needed were close at hand. Timber and water were readily available, as was stone for his chimney. The land was fairly level, for easy building and gardening. And he didn't have to be too concerned about boundaries or related legal bother. Almost any spot he picked was his. Of course, not all settlers had this kind of situation, but it did exist, and quite commonly.

Today, such a situation is utterly unheard of. You can hardly find a natural advantage, like stone, without finding it just where you don't want it, so you have to deal with the disadvantages as well as the advantages.

The pioneers were also used to working incredibly hard all their lives, in a way that few people today can equal. So while they just matter-of-factly put in a twelve-hour day at hard physical labor, most of us cannot do the same. To augment their own strength, they usually had a team of horses or oxen and a wagon for hauling logs and stone and other heavy work, and they were intimately familiar with handling them. Today, even if we could come by the team and wagon, few of us have the know-how to handle them, and in that case, look out! They're far more likely to haul you over the coals than to haul anything else for you.

The old-timers had advantages that we cannot possibly duplicate, but we, also have advantages that they lacked. The first and most valuable of these is information. Scientific and technological ideas and theories are available to the average person that were not dreamed of a hundred years ago, and we can use many of these advances when it comes to building a log cabin or any other home.

A second advantage we have over the old-timers is the common availability of money. The pioneers were better fitted to make what they needed, but most of us today are better able to buy it. Nor does the decrease in buying power due to inflation negate this. Although the actual price of food, clothing, and other articles has increased tremendously during the past century, the proportionate amount of our income that we pay for these items is much smaller than what our ancestors had to pay for the same items.

A third advantage today is the availability of manufactured goods. Such things as ready-made commercial roofing, floor tiles, and related articles were all but nonexistent then, even if a person did have money. Hinges, doors, tongue-and-grooved floor boards, and milled lumber could be bought in the cities, but not always on the frontier. What settlers usually could buy and transport were nails and windowpanes; they had to make just about everything else themselves.

A final advantage today stems from one of our biggest problems: waste. With so many waste materials everywhere, it is often easy to salvage them for use, while one hundred years ago there were comparatively few manufactured articles, and those were rarely wasted.

It is still possible to build a cabin from the bottom up, including all furnishings, without spending a penny on the structure, provided you already have a place to build, a source of water, sufficient timber, a few basic tools, and food. And throughout this book are directions for each stage of the operation according to this plan.

Not everyone will want to do this, however. If you have the choice of working to buy some of the materials for your cabin, or of making them yourself or making do without them, a little figuring on paper will help make it easier. Start by listing the simplest and cheapest ready-made articles, such as nails, screen, window plastic, and hinges, and moving on up to intermediate items, like a hand pump. Finish up with the more expensive ones, like a wood stove and ready-made sash or commercial roofing. List all the items that could make building notably easier for you and the end product more satisfactory. Itemize the cost of each, then compute how long you would have to work to pay for each at the wages you could expect (remember to deduct living expenses and taxes from your pay). When you have all these data, estimate how long it would take you to make the items yourself, double your estimate, and compare the two times. Finally, considering the probable times required, decide which you would be happier doing, or which things you would prefer to buy, and which others to make.

In a way, making this decision is similar to deciding to build a log cabin in the first place. Many people, when they want a house, work at a job, finance the house, and move in right away. It takes them twenty-five to thirty years to get it paid for, but they're living in it from the start. If you decide to build a log cabin, you can't live in it right away. If you can't buy many materials for it, aren't particularly skillful, and don't spend a lot of time every day working on it, it may be a year or more before it's done. But you own your own home from the day it's built.

Different people are happy doing different things, but to work out these lists for yourself and make up your mind, you need to be acquainted with certain tools, materials, and methods that can be used. So now we will begin to discuss them.

2
TOOLS, MATERIALS, AND METHODS

CUTTING TOOLS

Axes There are quite a few tools that could be useful in cabin-building. The first basic type of tool needed is an axe for felling trees. To many, the axe is the very symbol of the woods and the primitive life. It is the tool with which we picture lumberjacks felling giant trees amidst a background of rushing streams and conifers, the tool we see over the shoulders of the pioneers as they trudge westward. The axe is by far the most versatile all-around tool a person can have in dealing with primitive conditions and carving out a shelter.

It doesn't take a Paul Bunyan to use an axe efficiently, or great know-how and experience. What it does take is patience, and the willingness to go slowly enough to make each stroke count. An exceptionally weak person should not try felling a tree with one, but most people, with a little practice, can use a properly chosen axe to good advantage.

Choosing an axe takes some thought. Keep in mind that the axe for you is the one you can thoroughly control. You'll gain nothing by buying an axe too heavy for you with the idea that it will bite deeper. You'll only find out that it takes you twice as long to chop down a tree as with a lighter axe because you can't handle it properly.

If you intend to fell your trees with an axe, you should be a person of at least average strength; otherwise, it's better to use a Swedish saw. For most people, a good axe for felling is a single bit with a 2½-pound head, which usually comes with a 28-inch handle. You may want to change this handle for a longer one, up to 36 inches, depending on your arm length and how it feels to you. If you are exceptionally strong, or experienced in the use of an axe, you may find a 3½-pound single bit with a 36-inch handle more useful. But remember, unless you can also buy a smaller axe, the same axe will have to do both felling and notching, and for this combination, as well as for other jobs, the 2½-pound axe will be more versatile.

We recommend only single-bitted axes. Double-bits are not designed for the multiple uses to which an axe may need to be put during cabin-building, but are suitable only for extended chopping and splitting. The single-bit axe is a much more versatile tool. The best full-size axe we know of is the "Our Best" axe, made by Snow & Nealley of Bangor, Maine, and available from L. L. Bean, Freeport, Maine. It comes with either a 2½-pound or 3½-pound head. Collins is also a good and well-known brand, as is True-Temper.

When you buy your axe look for flaws in the head itself. Although technology today has the means to produce better steel than in the past, manufacturers sometimes take shortcuts and defects do occur. Look closely at the edge, too, to see if it is straight.

It used to be that when you bought an axe you had to have the blade thinned, but some brands have been thinned at the factory and don't seem to need it. A cheap hardware-store axe may well need it, however. If you sight along the edge and it hardly seems to come to a point at all, it needs it. The advantage of a thinned blade is that it will stand repeated sharpening without becoming a club too quickly, though eventually even a thinned blade will wear down. When this happens, have it reground on a manual grindstone, not an electric one, which would draw its temper.

Another thing to look for is how large the eye of the axe is, and the thickness of the metal surrounding it. Some brands have long, narrow eyes with thin metal surrounding. This causes two problems: the axe handles tend to keep snapping off at the head, and the thin metal walls can break more easily in cold weather when all metal is more brittle than usual.

Avoid handles made of ash, or those that are painted. Ash breaks too easily, and paint hides flaws. The best handles are straight and are made of hickory heart wood, which is dark in color. Watch out for knots in critical places, such as the middle of wide sides of the handle, since they may cause it to break. Small knots at the edges of the handle are acceptable, provided they are nowhere near the axe head. If the handle you buy is varnished, sand the varnish off because it will cause blisters.

Ideally, you should have two axes for cabin-building, the full-sized one for felling and other heavy work, and a light, pack-size axe with a 1½-pound head, single bit. This small axe is useful in a thousand ways, especially for notching up on the walls. In fact, for many, this axe plus a Swedish saw provides the ideal combination for felling and notching.

The same considerations apply to buying a small axe as to a large one, except that most small axes available seem to be of very middling quality. Norlund is a nationally known brand that fits this description. The quality is really nothing special, but neither is the price. We have had two of these for several years, and did most of the notching on our first cabin with them. They've held up like champions.

However, two new models of superlative quality have just appeared on the market. One is made by Estwing, and is one-piece, with head and handle of forged steel—no worrying about the handle ever breaking, unless you beat it on a rock. Since a metal handle will conduct much more of the shock of each blow to the hand and arm, the makers have coated the grip with tough foam that absorbs much of the shock and also insulates the hand when the axe is cold. This lifetime axe is lighter than an ordinary pack axe, and is of excellent design.

The other quality small axe is sold by L. L. Bean, and is called the Hudson Bay Cruising Axe. The "Hudson Bay" part refers to the shape of the head, which has a wide cutting edge, flaring out from an otherwise narrow head. The head weighs 1¾ pounds and comes with two choices of handle length, one 24 inches and the other 18 inches. Either would be extremely useful.

Swedish saw   If you don't feel you're up to felling with an axe, and can't afford or don't want a chain saw either, you can use the Swedish saw. Known also as a bucksaw, bow saw, or Sven saw, some form of this tool has been in use for centuries. It is a comparatively inexpensive tool and can make short work of all the felling and notching you need done.

Swedish saws come in assorted sizes, of which the most practical is the 30-inch blade. If you are building with softwood of fairly small diameter, you can probably expect the original blade and two extras to see you through, since they last a good while if you're not cutting hardwood. These also come in very light folding models, in case you might be packing in your possessions.

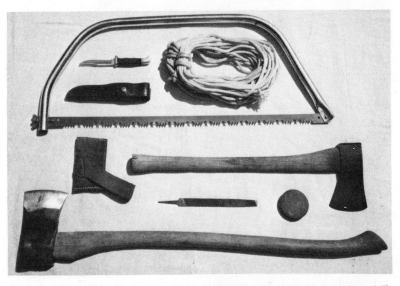

Cutting tools and accessories: full-size axe, sheath, file and axe stone, small axe, Swedish saw, rope, Buck knife and sheath.

A Swedish saw with two extra blades and a Norlund pack axe are a better bargain than one expensive axe. Also, if your blades get dull and you can't afford any more, you can resharpen them yourself. You have to do it by eye, and try to preserve the original angle of the blade. An ordinary triangular file is what we used, but a smaller file like the Bear Archery Razorhead sharpener might be more maneuverable. Neither is likely to do a really super job, but it took us about an hour, and lasted about a week. You can sneak by that way.

One-man/two-man saw   This is another option, if there are two of you. It says it can be used by one person, but this means one old-timer, not one modern. One person can just barely use it, but very slowly. Two people can use it very efficiently. You have to get into the rhythm of using it, with each person pulling in turn and neither pushing at all, or you'll damage the saw. You can resharpen this kind of saw with a special kit sold for the purpose. It takes a while to get accustomed to this saw if you're not an expert, but it is a lifetime tool.

If you are short on money, it would be more economical and faster, if there are two of you, to each use a Swedish saw. A one-man/two man saw sells for around $25, and two Swedish saws would cost the same or less.

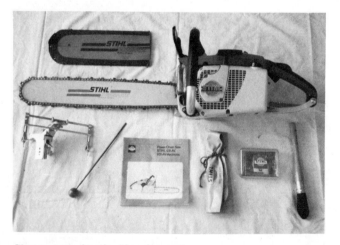

Chain saw, sheath, file, sharpening jig, cleaning brush, tool kit, manual.

Chain saw   When we were building our first cabin in Kentucky, located three quarters of a mile straight uphill and through the woods from the nearest road, we did not have a car. Then a generous relative gave us a chain saw, and we were flabbergasted and delighted. But the very first time we tried the chain saw, we broke something—and had no idea what. Then we discovered that the nearest place that did repairs and sharpening and carried chain saw supplies was thirty miles away. Since we had absolutely no cash or income, we couldn't even get it repaired.

A chain saw can be useful, especially if used in conjunction with the chain saw mill, described a little later. But it needs a lot of maintenance. It has to be thoroughly cleaned and sharpened each day of use. It also eats up gas, gasoline additive, and oil. If you can easily afford all the supplies and the unpredictable repairs, or can do them and the constant sharpening yourself (the sharpening takes about half an hour a day), a chain saw can really be a help. But otherwise, stick to an axe and manual saw.

CUTTING TOOL ACCESSORIES

With each of the above tools, certain accessories are necessary. With any axe, you need a 6- to 8-inch mill bastard file, and an axe stone. A Swedish saw, if you intend to sharpen it, needs a triangular file, or a Bear Razorhead file, as mentioned earlier. For a one-man/two-man saw, it takes either a 6- or 8-inch file plus a sharpening set. Chain saws take a rattail round file; the size will vary with the type of chain. These can be bought alone, but also come in a chain-saw accessory kit, which is worthwhile to have, if only for routine maintenance.

In felling with any saw, the blade sometimes becomes pinched by the weight of the tree, and you have to rescue it. For this you need a steel wedge and a heavy wooden maul or a sledge hammer or go-devil. There are also aluminum wedges, specifically for use with chain saws, but don't buy one for use with anything else because they don't function or hold up as well as steel. A sledge hammer or go-devil is used to beat the wedge into the tree. For living in the woods, it's a better idea to buy the go-devil, which is a sledge hammer on one end and a blunt-pointed log-splitter on the other. It will split anything!

If you can't afford to buy it, you can make a wooden maul out of a log section. Just take a 28- to 32-inch section of 4- to 6-inch hardwood (sized to fit your strength) and thin two-thirds of it with axe or hatchet so that it can be grasped easily by both your hands. Use the intact end to beat the wedge. For a superior product, cut a hardwood tree of the right diameter just below the ground level, where the small roots start to spread out. Use this end for a maul.

You also need something to measure with. A steel tape 100 feet long is best but can be rather expensive. Fifty feet or 25 feet will do fine, and anything is better than nothing. A 39¢ measuring tape made for sewing, 5 feet long, can be used. If all else fails, make knots in rope at 1-foot intervals.

Rope is a necessity. You need 50 to 100 feet of ¼- to ½-inch nylon or poly-propylene for purposes of safety in felling and for numerous other uses in building and woods living. This can be purchased cheaply in a discount house. The twisted polypropylene is considerably better than the braided, but costs almost twice as much. Polypropylene floats; nylon doesn't. Neither has very good abrasion resistance, but both are light for their strength, and they won't rot.

OTHER GENERAL AND WOODWORKING TOOLS

Twine   This is an inexpensive item that is indispensable and all-purpose, like rubber bands and safety pins; make every effort to have plenty of it.

Knife   Everyone who is building a cabin or living in the woods needs a knife. It has to be the sturdiest, most dependable, and versatile one that can be found, without regard to price. Many outdoors people have written that a kitchen knife bought at the five-and-ten makes an excellent woods knife, but the problem is that it doesn't do it for very long. While cheap knives may well skin game and cut up meat adequately, they aren't very satisfactory for wood-working. Such knives tend to break unless carefully handled, and ac-cidents are bound to happen sometimes.

A sheath knife designed for woods use is the best choice, but, on the other hand, you don't want one of those impressive-looking Bowie-type knives that are really too large and too thick for all-purpose use. What you do need, for building and other uses, is a 3- to 4½-inch blade, fairly rigid, but with some slight flexibility or it too will break easily. The handle is important. Many knives are equipped with bone handles or handles made of leather rings. Bone handles break easily, and the ones of leather rings often come apart. Either could perform well for you, but you're taking a chance. It's bet-ter to stick to a riveted wood handle or one of molded plastic.

An excellent knife for the purpose is the Buck Woodsman. Ours has a 3⅞-inch blade that can be used for all kinds of whittling, trimming, smoothing, skinning, butchering, all kitchen work, and countless other tasks. It sells for $16 most places, though we know of one discount house where you can get it for $12. It's really a very good bargain. Buck has the highest quality for the lowest price going. There are better knives, but the prices are much higher.

There are a couple of good quality knives that are a little less expensive. One is made by Olsen, and is called "Survival Knife." It is a good knife, for about $11, but it is large, with a 5½-inch blade, which can be a handicap. Another, for about the same price, is the Gerber "Pixie." It has a 3-inch blade and a molded plastic handle. It is almost too small, but it would just squeak by. A third alternative is called a Finnish Puuko knife, with a 3½-inch blade and simple wood handle, selling for about $8. This is probably the best alternative to a Buck Woodsman.

If you are really poor, look for a good medium-priced kitchen knife (about $4). Try to find the thickest blade available. Such a knife, with care, should last you long enough to build the cabin, though perhaps not much longer. But if you can possibly afford it, let a good knife be one of the top priorities.

Brace and augur bit   The alternative to using nails is pegging, and for every peg you need a hole. Using a brace and bit is the easiest way to make them. A good quality brace sells for $15 to $25 these days, and a poor one may fall apart on you. A ⅜- to ½-inch augur bit runs $4 or $5. That means $20 to $30 total if you have to buy them. The same money would buy quite a few nails, and nails are easier to use, so calculate closely how much you'd need to spend on nails as compared to the price of a brace and bit. Of course, the brace and bit will go on being useful long after the nails are used up, but you may not be able to afford the luxury of planning for the long run.

An alternative is an augur, which is a single bit on a long steel shaft, turned by a handle at the top. It's a lot more work, but if you can come by one for free in someone's barn, or cheaply at an auction, it's a lot better than nothing.

Hammer   If you're planning to use any nails at all in your cabin—for roofing, window frames, furniture, or whatever—a hammer is necessary. It is

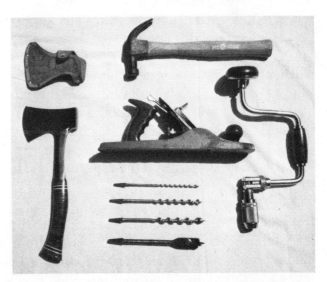

Estwing hatchet and sheath, hammer, handplaner, brace and bits.

true that you can carve a hammer out of hardwood, but it takes a while, and doesn't work as well. Hammers can be cheap, anyway, starting at about $2.

Estwing hatchet   This is not just another hatchet; it's in a category all by itself. Its construction is the same as the Estwing pack axe—solid steel—but is much smaller. There are two sizes: the larger about 13 inches long, and the smaller about 11 inches. The larger one seems better balanced. The handle is made of leather rings, anchored carefully so it won't come apart with use, and is shaped so that it fits the hand perfectly, and almost clings to it when chopping. This hatchet could be used for a fair amount of notching, smoothing, fitting, and furniture-making, not to mention splitting kindling later.

Chisel(s) and mallet   These are extremely useful, if you can afford the luxury of single-purpose tools. They can be used for several things, from smoothing a windowsill to carving out a groove for some tongue to fit in, to splitting out your notches instead of chopping. Although you can do these jobs with a small axe, hatchet, or knife, it is easier to do them with a chisel, so buy it if you can afford it, but don't worry if you can't.

Wood rasp   This rather inexpensive tool is really helpful in taking off splinters, rough-smoothing jagged edges, and the like. If you buy one of the old-fashioned solid ones, and not one with an open-work replaceable blade, it will last forever.

Handplaner   This is a carpenter's and cabinet-maker's tool for getting wood surfaces level and smooth. If you have both the finances and the inclination to make fine surfaces in finishing out the interior of your cabin, it is a must; otherwise, you don't need it.

Carpenter's saw   This is a generic term used to describe several different kinds of saws used in working finished lumber or plywood from a mill. They come with as few as five large teeth to the inch, for coarse work, on up to thirteen tiny teeth to the inch, for fine work. If you are likely to be using any such materials anywhere in the cabin, it's a good idea to have one. An eight-point saw is fairly versatile, as is a ten-point. Either extreme is likely to be too exclusive.

Drawknife   This is another tool for smoothing wood. Each of the various smoothing tools has its special areas where it is most useful on differently shaped and sized pieces. The drawknife's specialty is on boards not yet attached to anything, or on tool handles, and the like. If you can afford all of these assorted tools, by all means buy them because they'll come in very handy; but remember that the axe or hatchet or knife will also do all of these jobs to some extent.

Chain saw mill In case you are using a chain saw, here is something that will let you saw your own boards for a variety of uses instead of hewing or buying. Selling for $52 from the Brookstone Company of Peterborough, New Hampshire, it sets up fairly easily without altering your chain saw, and allows you to produce not only boards but beams and posts up to 12 feet long. There are other companies that make a similar device, but the Brookstone mill has a different design that seems to make it superior. It is supposed to work with any size saw, but it's pretty hard on the saw to use anything smaller than the equivalent of a Stihl 031 AV, and larger is better. Few saws other than circular saws like cutting with the wood grain, and that's what this is doing. Brookstone's address: 126 Vose Farm Road, Peterborough, New Hampshire 03458.

We have tried this, but the combined pollution and noise made us give it up. It's also very slow. But everyone may not be bothered by it.

SALVAGE TOOLS

For salvaging you will need a different set of tools. Here are the basic ones that should see you through just about anything in that line.

Tinsnips These are a necessity in converting most salvageable sheet metal and other heavy materials into useful pieces. Don't buy the huge persuaders, unless you're planning to cut up sheet iron, or your arm will fall off under continuous cutting. Buy the small, 8-inch-long size for most purposes, and the best quality you can afford. If you buy a cheap one, your arms and wrists will pay the extra price. If your snips get dull after much use, just get out your file and resharpen them, like any other cutting edge.

Hacksaw A hacksaw is useful for sawing through metal pipe or solid metal articles, as well as rubber tires. Blades have to be replaced, so buy spares.

Screwdriver This is the almost universal tool, even if you're not doing any salvaging at all. It's good for prying, stirring messes, scraping, and gouging, as well as screwing screws. Unless you can afford assorted sizes, choose a good medium-size one for all purposes.

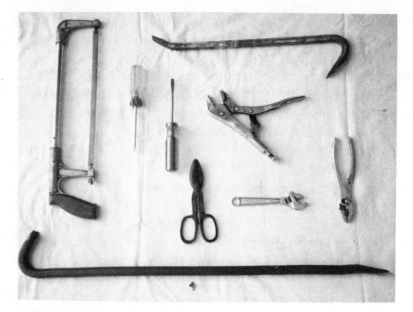

Salvage tools: large jimmy at bottom, small one at top, hacksaw at left, Phillips screwdriver and ordinary screwdriver, tinsnips, vise grips, small adjustable wrench, and pliers.

Phillips screwdriver You'll need one of these screwdrivers for all those screws that nearly everything salvageable is put together with. In fact you may need two of them, large and small, since there is a wide variance in the sizes of screws.

Jimmy This pulls nails, pries, pulls boards off buildings, and a dozen other useful things. A 2-½ or 3-foot length should suffice for most general salvage. The bigger the job, the bigger the jimmy.

Adjustable wrench Indispensable for everything.

Vise grips Sometimes it is almost impossible to make something hold still with one hand so the other hand can work on it. Here is the small hand tool that will do it, provided you buy a good quality one. A cheap one won't do anything.

Pliers For gripping anything and everything, loosening stubborn nuts, really essential for salvage.

Cold chisel For knocking off bolts and rivets, general cleaving, cutting metal in a pinch.

MISCELLANEOUS TOOLS

Ordinary shovel   It is possible to dig a hole with a pointed stick or pole, but any digging you do on the foundation is going to take much longer. It's far better to avoid digging altogether (see Chapter 4 on foundations for no-digging plans). A hint about digging with a shovel in heavy, clay soils: paint the shovel. Then the mud will not stick so terribly.

An alternative to an ordinary shovel is an army-type folding shovel. It's not any cheaper, but is smaller and lighter, so it can be packed in easier, if those are your circumstances.

Posthole digger   This tool is useful for digging foundation pits. It can also be used for sinking posts for various other purposes, but it isn't an absolute must in building.

There are two types, and both have advantages. The augur type operates by the drill principle, with the handle at the top being turned to dig. It's fast, sturdy, but sometimes has trouble with rocks. We prefer this kind, and clear obstructions out of the hole with a crowbar. The second kind clasps both its "hands" to remove dirt. It gets around small rocks better, but is less sturdy and not as fast, although it spits dirt out more easily.

Mattox   This is the trusty companion to the shovel, invaluable for many tasks, from digging through rocky clay or soil to cutting roots to planting a garden.

Crowbar   This, too, is mainly useful for the foundation. You can break rocks, pry rocks out of the ground, and tamp down soil with it. You can also split out bedrock in a well with it, but that's not really cabin-building. It's not one of the most necessary tools, though.

Wooden tamp   This you can make yourself if you need one. It can certainly help tamp and stabilize ground after digging pits for the foundation. The simplest kind is merely a 5-foot length of log, perhaps 6 inches thick, which you repeatedly lift and let fall on the area needing compacting. You can also attach a vertical handle to a horizontal puncheon, flat side down, and use it the same way.

Turf cutter   Also known as an edger, this is a specialty tool, useful mainly in cutting sod for roofing. It's not too expensive, and will help if you're planning to use sod. Many pioneers cut their sod with a sod plow pulled by their horses or oxen. If you happen to be in the situation where all these factors come together, by all means do the same.

Garden cart   This is useful for just about everything short of hauling the actual cabin logs. It will haul rocks for the fireplace or foundation, cinders, firewood, or groceries if you don't live near a road. It is not merely a wheelbarrow, nor the usual small-wheeled cart, but is an innovation by Garden Way Industries of Vermont. It has two bicycle-type wheels, and is balanced carefully to make it extremely stable and easy to pull, even when fully loaded. It comes in three sizes (the largest, which holds about 400 pounds, is the best). Ours has saved us a great deal of labor, but it is expensive— about $150. Contact Garden Way Research, Department 70074, Charlotte, Vermont 05445, for complete information.

Here's a list of all the most useful tools for cabin-building, with a price or price range next to each item. The asterisk indicates those tools that are absolutely essential.

CUTTING TOOLS

Axe, full-sized	$10 to $16
*Small axe	
Norlund	$8
Bean's	$11.75
Estwing	$18
*Swedish saw and two extra blades	$10 to $15
One-man/two-man saw	$25
Chain saw	$100 to $400

CUTTING TOOL ACCESSORIES

*6- to 8-inch mill bastard file	$1.25
*Axe stone	$3
*Triangular file	$1.25
Chain saw kit	$12
Steel wedge	$4.25
Sledge hammer	$15
Go-devil	$15
*Measuring tape	39¢ to $13
*Rope—100 feet of ¼-inch polypropylene	$2.99 to $5

OTHER GENERAL AND WOODWORKING TOOLS

*Twine—400 feet of 121-pound-test nylon	$1.66
*Knife	$4 to $16

*Brace and augur bit (or nails)	$20 to $30
Hammer	$2 to $15
Estwing hatchet	$10 to $12
Chisel(s) and mallet	$6
Wood rasp	$3
Handplaner	$12 to $15
Carpenter's saw, Disston 8-point	$6.60
Drawknife	$8 to $12
Chain saw mill	$52

SALVAGE TOOLS

Tinsnips—8 inch Wiss	$4.95
Hacksaw	$2 to $5
Screwdriver	$1.29
Phillips screwdriver	$1.29
Jimmy—36 inch	$3
Adjustable wrench, small	$4.32
Vise grips	$4 to $8
Pliers	$3 to $5
Cold chisel	$2

MISCELLANEOUS TOOLS

Ordinary shovel	$5 to $25
Army folding shovel	$5
Posthole digger	$15
Mattox	$10 to $15
Crowbar	$15.66
Wooden tamp	—
Turf cutter	$4 to $9
Garden cart	$75 to $150

From this list you can compile one that will fit your circumstances. If you add up the items marked with an asterisk, you will note that the minimum total outlay is going to be in the neighborhood of $50 to $55. If you can spend only $20 to $30 more than this, we would not recommend using it for additional tools, but rather that you buy clear plastic and screen for your windows with it, and some small nails to attach them with. Money so spent will buy you more convenience under the circumstances than the same amount spent any other way.

In essence, then, $100 will certainly buy all your tools and materials for the poverty-stricken plan. Then all you need are the place to build, timber, water, and food. You may not have to spend even $100, since most people know someone from whom they can beg or borrow at least some of these tools. There are also auctions, where you might be able to pick up an old axe, shovel, mattox, posthole digger, and crowbar for maybe $10, in one lot. So keep your eyes open. All else failing, remember to go to discount houses to buy most tools. Usually you can find excellent quality for much less money, if you look carefully and examine the tools. The typical hardware store is probably the most expensive place to buy tools, so avoid it if at all possible.

MATERIALS

COMMERCIAL MATERIALS

You may want to use some commercial materials somewhere in your cabin, so for easy reference we're including this list of some of the most common ones. The prices listed here are from a local lumber mill not far from a large city, and are from the summer of 1977.

Exterior Plywood—4×8-foot sheet

¼-inch A.C. good one side	$ 8.85
⅜-inch A.C. good one side	$11.44
½-inch A.C. good one side	$13.76
⅝-inch A.C. good one side	$15.96
¾-inch A.C. good one side	$19.40

Interior Plywood (not birch)—4×8-foot sheet

¼-inch A.D. good one side	$ 7.92
⅜-inch A.D. good one side	$11.69
½-inch A.D. good one side	$14.57
⅝-inch A.D. good one side	$16.94
¾-inch A.D. good one side	$20.34

CDX Plywood

⅜-inch	$ 7.30
½-inch 3-ply	$ 8.30
½-inch 4-ply	$ 8.95
¾-inch	$12.16

Particle Board
⅝-inch	$ 4.96
¾-inch	$ 8.65

Fiberboard
½-inch sheet-insulation board	$ 2.72

Two-by-fours
8-foot economy	$ .69
8-foot good grade	$ 1.40
12-foot good grade	$ 2.11

Tar Paper—per roll
90 pound	$ 7.70
60 pound	$ 5.64
30 pound	$ 7.90

Brick—cheapest—per thousand $96.00

Cement per bag $ 2.96

Cement block—each $ .36

Aluminum screen—36 inches wide—per foot $ .45

Window plastic—36 inches wide, clear, per foot $ .48

Creosote—5-gallon can $11.00

Hinges
3-inch brass loose pin, for windows or cupboards —pair	$ 1.89
3-inch zinc plate, for screen or storm doors—pair	$ 1.69
Barn hinges—each	$ 5.00

Dowel rods—birch—36 inches
¼ inch	$ .12
⅜ inch	$ .20
½ inch	$ .25
⅝ inch	$ .35
¾ inch	$ .65

Nails

Common nails are 45¢ a pound. This can mean drastically varying numbers of nails depending on size. Here are the number of nails per pound of the ones we counted:

10-penny	57 to the pound
16-penny	46 to the pound
20-penny	28 to the pound
40-penny	16 to the pound
60-penny	10 to the pound

The smaller sizes and roofing nails were too numerous to count. But ¾-inch roofing nails sold for 65¢ a pound.

METHODS

USING AN AXE

This is almost a lost art, so here are some basics to help get you started.

To swing an axe, stand with your feet well apart, so you feel very stable. Grasp the axe halfway down the handle with your lead hand, and your other hand near the butt. Swing it back and up until it's extended at arm's length above and behind your lead shoulder, then just continue the motion in a circle and it will begin to fall forwards and down. This is the time to direct it with very slight movements of your hands. Remember that the whole movement should be effortless, once you start it going, with the axe's own weight doing all the work. The swing should be rhythmic and gentle, not forced. Practice will perfect this.

The axe head must bite into the wood at an angle of 45 degrees or less, not straight in, or it will never cut anything. Never work nervously or get out of breath. If this happens, you are trying to put too much force into it, or you have an axe too heavy for you. Accuracy counts, not speed. This, too, will improve with practice.

You need to learn to swing from both shoulders, since a notch, whether in felling or fitting, is cut from both sides. Make your notch wide enough to begin with, or you'll find yourself with no place to chop. This is hard to picture, but most beginners discover the problem. To avoid trouble, make the area you're removing as wide or tall as the log is thick.

When you're chopping an already-felled log in two, stand on one side and chop on the other, so that the thickness of the log is between you and any misstroke. Never chop on top of a log, except when notching it up on the walls.

There is a pattern of strokes that will let you chop a log in two most easily. If you have perfected your swing and aim, and used this pattern, the whole round chip should lift out in one piece. When this is done, stand on the opposite side and do the same on the unfinished side. After that big chip is removed, a stroke or two should sever the log. The reality of doing all this is much simpler than it sounds.

Axes can be dangerous as well as useful, and most people don't take axe safety seriously enough. Here are a few safety rules that we hope you will follow:

- When chopping, make sure your area of swing is well cleared of brush and branches—an axe always reaches farther than you think.
- Make sure you have the proper length axe handle for you. If you don't, the axe may miss the log and sink into you instead of the ground.
- If you have to chop with a small axe, with approximately a 20-inch handle, try kneeling down to do it. But spread your knees well apart, and be alert.

- Always be sure the log itself is lying stable before beginning to chop.
- Don't let anyone stand nearby, whether cat, dog, or human. Axeheads do fly off the handle occasionally, and handles break.
- Keep your axe sharp, and always covered with a leather sheath that has its edge riveted as well as sewn. This means *always*, when not in use, including just carrying it from the site to the tree. If it's not covered and you stumble on some brush, or the dog runs between your legs, you could be dead.
- Be continually alert to move out of the way if your axe glances off what you're chopping.
- Take time to rest. This is safer, guarantees greater efficiency, and saves axe handles.
- Park your axe properly when it's not in use. This means leaned against a tree with its sheath on, or stuck firmly into a stump where you're not likely to bump into it. No edges exposed.

AXE SHARPENING

Rough-sharpening an axe is fairly easy, though some may disagree. Here's the method that works for us. Sit on a rock, stump, or chair and place the axehead on one knee, with the handle extending down under your other knee. Apply pressure downward with the second knee until the axe can scarcely move.

With the axe head lying flat on your knee, its edge turned away from you, push the file across the edge away from the blade with your lead hand, holding the axe head firmly with your other hand. Watch the light reflecting on the blade as you sharpen. When it shines evenly all along the edge, you

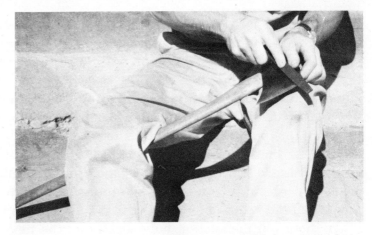

One way to hold the axe steady to sharpen it.

are through with that side. Turn it over, switch knees, and do the other side the same way, being careful not to take off any more metal on one side than on the other. Remember to push the file in only one direction, and never drag it back again. Lift it instead.

Now you can finish it up with a round composition axe stone that fits in the palm of the hand. A circular, scouring motion is used, beginning at each corner of the blade, and going to the center of it, but let the stone grind only during the outward stroke. Lift on the return stroke, just as in filing, or the axe will grow duller, not sharper.

Some people have difficulty in telling when the blade is considered sharp. The Vikings used to be able to shave with theirs, but otherwise you can tell by how the light strikes the blade, and by the thickness of the pointed edge when you hold it up and sight along it. A sharp axe is comparatively thin pointed, while a dull one is more chisel-shaped. And, of course, a sharp blade cuts well and holds its edge.

HEWING

In the woods, flat surfaces, such as boards, simply do not occur naturally. Since flat surfaces are invaluable in nearly any operation, they have to be made. The simplest way to get one is to split a log in two, and smooth the two semiflat surfaces that result. These smoothed half-logs are called puncheons. They are limited in their usefulness because it is practical to produce them only 3 feet long or less. At this length, they can be made by simply standing the log on end and splitting it with axe or go-devil like firewood, but to split a longer log you have to lay it on its side and use axe, wedges, and sledge hammer. With today's wood, it is a lengthy and laborious process.

For longer pieces, or for space conservation, it is better to produce slabs, or thick rough boards, by hewing. This, too, is some work, but not disproportionate. Start with a log the length of the board you want, and as thick, too, if possible. Then estimate how much wood you must remove on both top and bottom to arrive at the board you want, and either mark the log or proceed by eye. Now cut a series of lopsided V-notches to the correct depth, all along the top of the log, at 1-foot intervals or less. To make these, make the slanting cut first, then the vertical cut to knock out the chip. If using a saw, make the vertical cuts first with the saw, then the slanting cuts with the axe, to knock the chip out. When all the Vs are made, take the axe and strike a hard blow along the slanting side of the first one, into the base of the V. This will either knock out the section between it and the next V, or will loosen it so the next blow will do the job.

When you have made that whole side flat, you can use it as is, like a puncheon, for various jobs, such as flooring, or you can turn it over and hew off the other side, too. Remember that all the chunks you hew off are firewood. When you're finished hewing, you can smooth it with the axe or any other tool you may have.

PIT-SAWING

There is another way of producing boards, by pit-sawing, which was used by the Colonials, but this is also very laborious and requires two persons and a set-up as well. We do not recommend it for the average person, and are not including instructions. If you're interested in more information about pit-sawing, see Edwin Tunis's *Colonial Living* (World Publishing Company), and Eric Sloane's *A Museum of Early American Tools* (Funk & Wagnalls).

PEGGING

The Colonials had pegging down to an art. Pegs were highly respected by them even if they had nails, because pegs lasted longer and held firmer if properly done. There were several ingenious ways to make sure a peg held, even after it had shrunk, and throughout varying weather conditions.

One was the use of a square peg in a round hole. The hole was drilled, and the peg was carefully whittled so that its diagonal measurement was a little larger than the hole's diameter. Then, if the peg was green, it could be beaten in with a maul, but if seasoned, it was first greased so it would slide more easily, and then beaten in.

Another way was to make an ordinary round peg larger than the hole, and grease and beat it in the same way. Sometimes, too, a round peg of seasoned wood was whittled to an exact snug fit and barbs were very carefully whittled all over it, so that it would beat in easily, but the barbs would prevent its working out again later.

They would also sometimes drill holes, which didn't quite line up, in two items to be pegged together. Then when a peg was pounded in, the crookedness resulting would make it stay put.

These are valuable techniques to remember, though they take patience, and may come in handy in building. For the most part, though, just drilling a hole and whittling a peg to fit it will do fine. Always make the peg snug, especially with green wood, but don't get too greedy or the article you're pegging may split on you.

For pegs, green hardwood of a tight and twisty grain is best, such as hard maple, sycamore, black gum, dogwood, hawthorn, yellow birch, or beech. Seasoned wood is better for furniture. Softwoods can also be used, especially if no great pressure will be on them, as in attaching slabs for a roof. For such uses as pegging rungs on a ladder, use the very best wood you have. Birch dowel rods are excellent, too, and inexpensive.

MAGIC CEMENT

Here is a formula for a homemade cementlike mixture that has been used to chink cabins, and can be used for many other purposes just as well.

> 2 parts clay or dirt (sifted as finely as possible)
> 1 part sifted wood ashes
> ½ part salt (granulated, not rock)
> Water to mix (as little as possible)

This should be mixed just wet enough to spread without too much trouble, so add the water cautiously.

It has many uses—as a roofing material, as firebrick in a fireplace or stove, or as the entire article if made into bricks. It can be used as bricks for the walls of small outbuildings. To make bricks, you need only one mold. Just tap out each brick while still damp. It can even be useful in making large stationary containers for dry storage, such as crocks, bins, etc. It will work as plaster for walls or ceiling, and can be applied over rough surfaces to produce a comparatively smooth one. And it is a fairly good mortar.

RUBBER TIRES

This is a first-quality salvageable material that is widely available and good for countless uses. You can use it for roofing, for making springy surfaces in furniture, for mounting glass in windows instead of points, and sealing out drafts around windows and doors. Among other things, it can be made into flashing on roofs, and into very strong, silent hinges. The uses are limited only by your imagination.

PINE PITCH

Although it's usually called "pine" pitch, it can be made from any of the needle-leaf evergreen trees native to this country. To make it, first collect the lumps of pitch found on wounds on such trees. If you can't find any lumps, you can score the tree's bark clear through the inner bark and attach containers to catch what runs out. Scrape off what hardens there, too. Take the lumps and boil them in water for fifteen minutes, skimming what rises to the surface, then reheat that skimming to use it. Apply it as you would tar. Some say the result is better if you mix a small amount of grease with it, and heat them together before using.

Another way to make it is to burn wood on a sloping rock or a tilted flat container. The pure pitch will run out of the wood, and can be collected at the bottom of the sloping surface.

This product is good for general waterproofing, for daubing of seams, and for use as glue.

3
DESIGN AND SPECIFICATIONS

Like any home, a log cabin should be carefully planned and personalized to your needs. All the activities connected with daily living take place inside the cabin, so it has to be able not only to handle them but to make them as easy as possible.

Many people don't think of log cabins in the same way they think of ordinary modern houses. Frequently they just pick a size and build it, then try to fit everything they want in afterwards. The problem with this is that you can't always fit in the things you want, or even if it all fits, it may be so inconvenient that you have to be constantly running back and forth. You might even build it too big, and you end up occupying only a corner of it.

The only way to avoid costly waste of time and materials is to decide upon the size you need before you build. The shape, too, makes a difference. A square with a certain amount of floor space will sometimes just not hold the furnishings that a rectangle with the same floor space will, and vice versa.

We have used only squares and rectangles in our sample plans, because they are the only practical shapes for a log cabin. Logs are a rigid material, best adapted to straight lines. It's possible to produce odd shapes, such as octagons, by abutting the logs at large angles, but this is incredibly more difficult than the conventional shapes, as we found by building an octagon. The notches are much harder to chop, and there are twice as many of them. The inside is also very poorly adapted to efficient organization. We emphatically do not recommend them.

There are certain general considerations that any dwelling should meet. It must be dry when it is wet outdoors, and cool and shady in hot weather. The roof provides these things automatically. The inside should be as light and airy as it is possible to make it. A cabin cannot have too many or too large windows. The windows shown in our plans were usually the largest we could fit in, but you can reduce them if you are limited by money or time.

The cabin should also feel spacious, not closed in, even though it should actually be no larger than necessary. A one-room cabin offers the most spacious feeling and the best possibilities for space organization. For these reasons, virtually all of our plans are for one-room cabins, ranging from tiny to quite large.

How can you know *exactly* how much space, and what shape, you need? You start by determining what furnishings and fixtures you'll need, and how big they are, then experiment with plans until you come up with one that will hold everything in a convenient and pleasing way. This can take a lot of time if you've never done it before, and that is why we have included so many sample plans. Probably no one will build any of them exactly, but they can give a good idea of what will fit into a given space. More than anything else, you have to build your cabin on the basis of the kind of life you are going to live.

You may be thinking of equipping your cabin with modern conveniences. You will have little difficulty designing a cabin with that in mind, since these often take up less space than their counterparts made from wood. The only disadvantage is that it can get complicated if you want a lot. We are going to concentrate on items made from wood since they are less commonly understood and since most people interested in cabin-building will want to know about them.

In the woods all the services are provided by you, rather than by electricity, gas, or plumbing from outside sources. In place of a stove for cooking and a furnace for heating, a single wood stove or fireplace is used for both. Instead of electric light, you have firelight and homemade candles or kerosene lamps. Water doesn't come from faucets, it comes in buckets, and you soon learn to conserve it to save carrying more than you have to. You get it hot by heating it over the fire, and wash your dishes in dishpans placed on the table.

Your food isn't stored in a refrigerator or freezer, but in a large closet full of shelves, called the pantry, or in a springhouse. Your dishes and cooking utensils are kept there, too. Unless you are a large family who needs auxiliary counters, your working surface is the same table you eat at, and both table and pantry are placed near fireplace or stove for easy access.

Your everyday clothing can be hung in a closet, or it can be folded in a chest. But you need someplace to put muddy clothes and boots just inside the door, since you get dirty a lot in the woods and you don't want to track mud any more than necessary.

A virtual necessity in the woods is some sort of easy chair for relaxation. The pioneers didn't usually have them, but then they just never sat down. If they weren't working or eating they were sleeping. The modern person, however, is likely to find himself sorely hurting without one, especially since we have been trained to need and expect quiet relaxation. The easy chair can be either a permanent or folding chair, depending on what is comfortable and acceptable to you, but you should have space for one chair, or perhaps couch-space equivalent, for each adult. (For some reason children do not seem to feel a need for such amenities.) If you expect company, and want to provide for it, spare folding chairs will do fine if there is space to set them up.

Naturally you will need a bed of some kind. Make sure it's big enough. You're more active in the woods, and you will need to really stretch out and sleep well. When a person lies flat and stretches his arms out above his head, with his feet extended, he adds 1½ feet to his height. But even then, it is not pleasant to have your hands and feet encounter walls, so add at least another 6 inches to that. Two feet plus height is a good length for beds. The beds we've shown are 2½×8 feet for one person, and 4×8 feet to 5×8 feet for two people.

Toilet facilities in the woods amount to either an outhouse or one or more chamberpots, or combination thereof. We personally think that an outhouse is the worst possible way of dealing with the problem, since they are obnoxious all the time and have to be cleaned out or moved periodically as well.

Far better is the plan of using one or more chamberpots, and carefully composting the contents each day. This may be done by adding the contents to the garbage compost heap, and covering with a little hay or dirt each time, or it may be done according to a method developed by Sir Albert Howard, the pioneer of English organic gardening. His research showed that if a pile of loose dirt were made and a depression scooped in its top, human wastes could be dumped on it every day, and the liquid would immediately be absorbed by the earth, while the solids remaining would rapidly dry out from sun and wind. The pile would be virtually odorless, and the immediate absorption of the liquid would allow the earth to retain all of the nitrogen in it, while the solids would rapidly break down. In a comparatively short period of time, the entire pile would turn into amazingly rich fertilizer for the garden, and would not breed insects in the meantime.

This plan requires no time spent in construction, costs nothing as opposed to plumbing, and wastes neither water nor fertilizer, and it is entirely in harmony with nature, since it follows as closely as possible the same process that every other animal on earth uses. The only cautionary measure is to keep it some distance from the water supply.

So the list of necessary furnishings comes down to these: fireplace and/or stove, pantry, table and benches or stools, easy chair, closet and/or chest, bed, and chamberpots. This isn't really very much.

The sample plans are more or less divided under the headings of One Person, Two People, Five People, and Ten People, but in some cases they overlap, and this is discussed. The plans are drawn to a scale of ¼ inch = 1 foot. The furnishings are adequate in size to the number of people planned for.

The fireplaces shown in all the plans are supposed to be the fireplace-stove we designed (for details, see Chapter 8), but a wood stove could be substituted in most cases. A fireplace built entirely within the walls is more efficient thermally than one built on the outside of a wall, but in some of the smallest plans it is shown on the outside because we found it impossible to do otherwise. However, in those instances, the cabins are so tiny that a backpacking stove would almost heat them, so the fireplace even on the outside will be more than adequate.

ONE PERSON

We're starting at the small end rather than the large because dealing with a small space can give you more of an idea what can be done with a larger one. Much of the inspiration here came from concepts of trailer organization, so you'll probably be surprised to see how little space is actually necessary.

The first two plans for one person are what we call emergency plans. The idea is that you can build one of these to get under shelter quickly, then build the permanent cabin at your leisure.

PLAN 1

Plan 1 suggests the inside of a hollow tree because of its smallness. The bed is 8 feet long and 2½ feet wide, which ought to accommodate even a very large person. Above the head of the bed are several pegs upon which to hang pajamas in the morning and the day's clothes at night. Beginning about 2 feet above the foot of the bed are shelves going up to the ceiling for books or miscellaneous small items. These could be replaced, in the case of a fully grown but nonetheless very small adult, by a closet 1½-feet deep, opening on the bed.

Beside the bed is a window so that the morning light can wake the occupant. The bed itself is used as a couch in the daytime. Underneath the whole length of the bed the wood for the fireplace is stored, and over the bed at a height of 6 to 6½ feet is a shelf the same size as the bed, for storage of clothing and personal belongings.

Adjacent to the bed, but separated from it by a pole partition (shown in the drawing as a curved line), is the 3×2½-foot table. It is so situated that the person eating sits looking out the window. Under the table dishpans can be hung on the wall without interfering with the person's legs. On the other side of the table is the pantry, with pole walls and a door. More wood can be stored under the shelves if needed.

The cabin door is 2½ feet wide, with pegs on the back for hanging up wet and muddy coats, and next to the door is space for placing wet boots. There is a small window beside the door to give light for working at the fire.

The fireplace opening is 3 feet wide and 1½ feet deep, sufficient for the short-term cooking needs of up to two people, and a stone hearth 1½ feet deep runs the width of the fireplace to prevent danger from sparks. A person in a hurry could use the temporary stone camp stove shown in Chapter 8 until he has time to build the fireplace, or he could just dispense with the fireplace entirely.

There is room in the center of the cabin to set up a folding chair before the fire, but the bed-as-couch would probably be sufficient.

PLAN 2

This plan is slightly larger, 8×10 feet. The bed is the same as in Plan 1, with a shelf above and wood storage below. There is also a clothes closet opening above the head of the bed, and a pantry that is twice the size of the one in Plan 1. This is a definite improvement, since it is almost impossible to have too large a pantry. It is a priceless catchall, as well as performing its other duties.

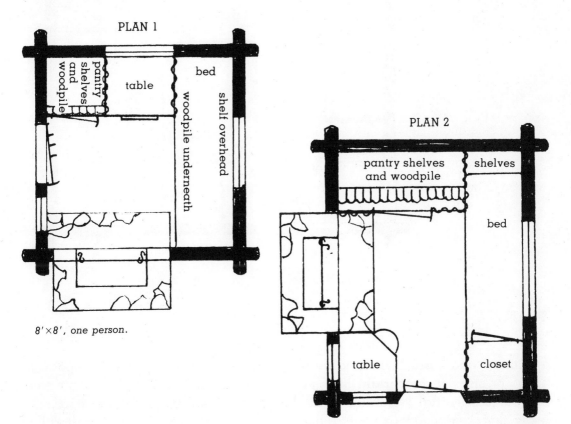

PLAN 1

pantry shelves and woodpile

table

bed

woodpile underneath

shelf overhead

8'×8', one person.

PLAN 2

pantry shelves and woodpile

shelves

bed

table

closet

8'×10', one person.

PLAN 3

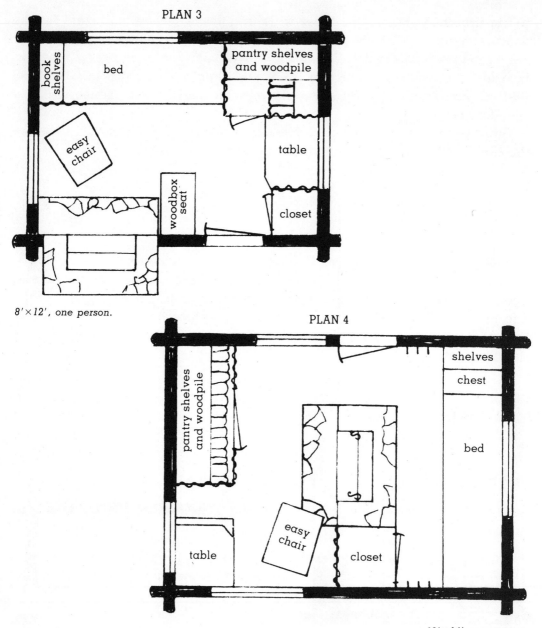

8'×12', one person.

PLAN 4

10'×14', one person.

PLAN 3

Plans 3 and 4 are both suitable for permanent homes for a single person (if he or she can be certain of remaining so). Plan 3 is 8×12 feet, and has the same essential features as Plan 2 but with the addition of a permanent easy chair and woodbox seat on the other side of the fireplace, permitted by the roomier center space.

PLAN 4

The design for this cabin is considerably larger and of a different design than the others. It is 10×14 feet, and offers a separate bedroom containing the bed with shelf overhead and wood underneath, a closet, several pegs, and at the foot of the bed either a large chest with shelves above or a second closet 2×2½ feet in size.

The fireplace is entirely inside, since there is room for it here, and the back of it functions as a room divider and warms the bedroom.

The rest of the cabin is a little kitchen–living room, with a large pantry, easy chair, log stool, and table with bench. The wall of the pantry acts as a back to the bench, so the person eating can lean back.

TWO PEOPLE

PLAN 5

Here again, both Plans 5 and 6 would be considered emergency plans. Plan 5 is 10×10 feet. It is actually just an expanded version of the one-person 8×10. The bed is 4½ feet wide, with a 2×4½-foot closet at the head and shelves above the foot. A 2½-foot shelf runs the length overhead, and wood storage is underneath. There's also a large pantry, a small table, and a door with pegs on the back for wet coats. A large window is over the bed, and two small ones at the table. The fireplace is 3×1½ feet. Since the sleeping is downstairs, this cabin could be built with a shallow lean-to roof for speed of construction.

PLAN 6

This plan is also 10 feet square, but here the sleeping is upstairs, so a roof pitch of at least 45 degrees or a gambrel would be necessary. It is somewhat more spacious, with a larger table and benches, regular large pantry, and two permanent easy chairs. Clothing storage is upstairs with the bed.

PLAN 7

Plan 7 is 10×16 feet and is an expansion of the 10×14 for one person. This could be either an emergency cabin or a permanent one, depending upon what you like. The beds are bunk beds, and there are two permanent easy chairs, a larger table with benches, and a pantry in the kitchen–living area.

If you like this cabin, but prefer a double bed, just add two feet on to the bedroom end, making it 10×18 feet, and a double bed will fit.

PLAN 5

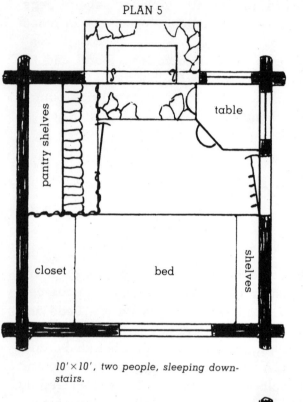

10'×10', two people, sleeping downstairs.

PLAN 6

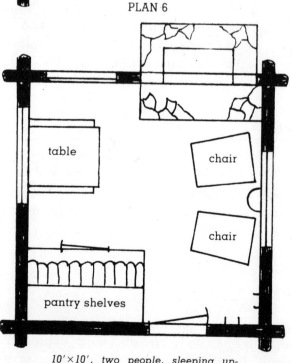

10'×10', two people, sleeping upstairs.

PLAN 7

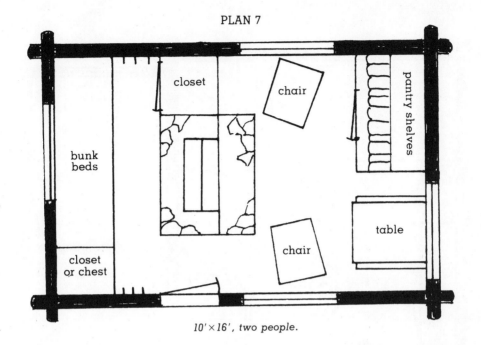

10'×16', two people.

PLAN 8

Plan 8 shows our second cabin, which was to be an emergency one but had to be suitable for at least two years occupancy, and also had to provide a place to write. It is 12-foot square, with a lean-to shed added on. Starting on the south side is the front door, 2½ feet wide, with several pegs on the back. To its right are the water buckets along the wall, and the stove, 1½ feet from the wall. Farther along the wall is a 6×4 window, and under it in the southeast corner is the 3-foot-square table. A 3×4-foot window is around the corner on the east wall, and a lamp is hanging on the wall between it and the back door, leading into the shed.

Beyond the door is the 4×4½-foot pantry. Jutting into the pantry is the back of a clothes closet whose front opens at the head of the bed adjacent on the north wall. The closet occupies a space only 4 feet high, from 18 inches up to 5½ feet, so there is storage in the pantry both above and below the closet. Next, the bed, 8×4½ feet, with a 4×4-foot window on the wall above it. There is an over-bed shelf, the same size as the bed, at a height of 5½ feet, and bookshelves cover the wall above the bed's foot. Under the bed are stored the washtub, galvanized bathtub, laundry bag, and clean boots. At the bed's lower outside corner a ladder rises to the attic, and also provides access to the nether reaches of the over-bed shelf. Above the ladder is a trapdoor large enough to raise or lower large items on a rope.

Beyond the ladder on the west wall is a 4-foot-square window with the writing desk beneath. The desk's foldout leaf clears the stove with plenty of room. Adjoining the desk in the southwest corner is a coat closet, right inside the front door.

PLAN 8

N

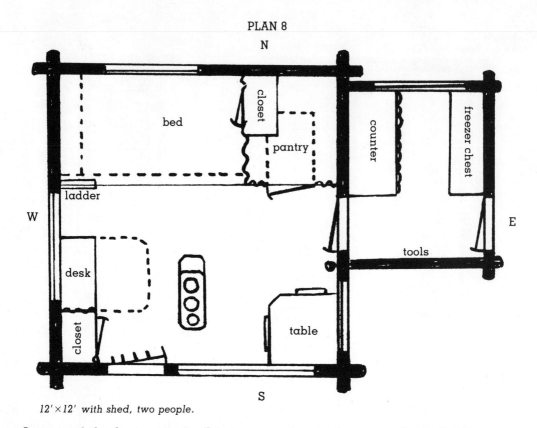

W   E

S

12'×12' with shed, two people.

In one of the large empty floor spaces is another trap door giving access to the small 4-foot-square root cellar beneath the floor. And there is room to set up two folding chairs for relaxing, as well as the bed being usable as a couch.

In the shed, tools hang along the south wall, and on the north wall is a 4-foot-square window to give light to the 2×4½-foot counter, where butchering, grain-grinding, and other rough jobs are done. Under the counter, the woodpile is stored. Opposite the counter on the outside east wall is the freezer chest, made as described later in this chapter.

PLANS 9 and 10

Both plans are 16-feet square. We have found this size to be more versatile than almost any other in adapting to different types of arrangement.

These are the first plans where there is enough juggling room to pay much attention to cardinal directions, which can be an important consideration for a permanent home. It is desirable to have large windows along a south wall, to provide maximum light and heat during the winter. Taking advantage of the sun in this way can save you a lot of wood. This heating potential can be amplified by stoning in a patio on the south side beneath those large windows, to catch and hold the day's heat.

East is the side where it is nice to have the dining table, so as to get the early morning light when eating breakfast, and be relatively cool for the rest of the day. It is also a good direction to have a window over the bed, to awaken early with the sun.

West, or south and west, is the best side to place the easy chairs for reading and relaxing; the light lingers there the longest, and most people tend to do most of their relaxing at the end of the day. And north is the best side for the fireplace, and for the dining, kitchen, or bedroom windows if you can't get them on the east.

Plan 9 meets most of these qualifications. It is for two people who like a lot of space, and plan to sleep upstairs. The fireplace is in the center of the north wall. It is a larger one than in the previous plans because in the long run, two people need a fireplace 4 feet wide and 2 feet deep, for cooking, heating, hot water production, canning, etc. The pantry is to the right of the

PLAN 9

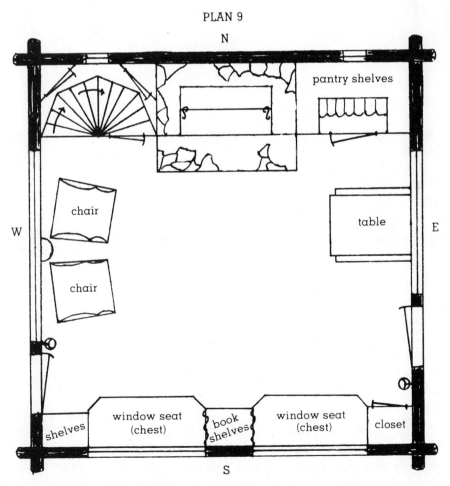

16'×16', two people, sleeping upstairs.

PLAN 10
N

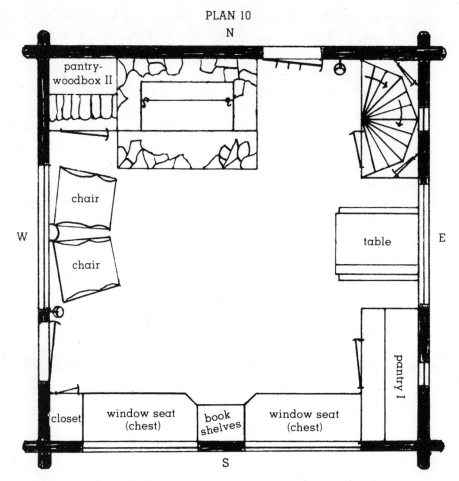

16'×16', two people, rearranged.

fireplace, and the staircase to the left. (See Chapter 9, "Finishing Up," for how to build.) Under the stairs is a small closet, perhaps for kindling. The whole effect is of a completely paneled wall.

Along the west wall is an 8×4-foot window, and the two large easy chairs. Next is the back door, with a lantern hanging on a peg inside for easy grabbing when you go out in the evening.

On the south wall are two 5×5-foot windows, with a bookcase between them. Beneath each window is a wide window seat with storage underneath. In the southwest corner are more shelves, and in the southeast corner is a small coat closet.

The east wall holds the front door, also with lantern-peg adjacent, for easy lighting when returning to a dark house at night, and a 6×4-foot window with the table and benches beside it.

Plan 10 is just a rearrangement of Plan 9, included mainly to show how these plans can frequently be juggled if you like some parts but not others, or if the cardinal directions don't work out right with your site.

PLAN 11

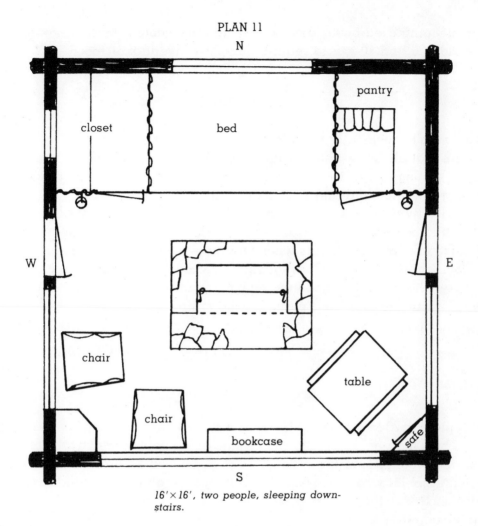

16'×16', two people, sleeping downstairs.

PLAN 11

This plan is also 16-foot square, but here the sleeping is downstairs. The bed is 5×8 feet, in the center of the north wall. As in previous plans, a 2½-foot shelf runs the length overhead, and wood is stored beneath. Separated from the bed on either side by pole partitions are a large closet 4×5 feet and a pantry of the same size. The closet has its own small window for light.

Adjacent to the closet on the west side is the front door, and then a 5×4-foot window behind one easy chair. In the southwest corner is a small table holding a lamp, and next to it on the south wall the other easy chair. Along the south wall is a 12-foot window, running partly behind one easy chair. There is a bookcase beneath it beside that chair, and the table set across the southeast corner, with a small safe for dishes in that corner itself. The east wall has a 5×4-foot window and a back door. The fireplace is in the center with free passage around it. The whole effect of the inside is somewhat circular, because of the arrangement of the furniture.

The sleeping area being downstairs, this plan could have a lean-to roof, while Plans 9 and 10 would require steeper conventional roofs.

FIVE PEOPLE

We haven't specifically included any plans for the family of five because we think that all three 16-foot squares are adaptable to them, if the roof is at least 45 degrees or a gambrel. This should provide plenty of sleeping space for just the children or for parents and children.

After all, living in the woods isn't the same as the city or suburbs. In the woods, bedrooms are not a place to relax, but only to sleep. Relaxing and recreation take place outdoors whenever the weather permits, and in the living room when it doesn't. Consequently, bedrooms needn't be so elaborate. For those who think they need more space than the 16-foot-squares provide, take a look at the following plans for the family of ten.

TEN PEOPLE

PLAN 12

This plan is 20-foot square. It has a 4×2-foot fireplace on the east wall, flanked by a high-backed settle on one side and a pantry specifically for pots, pans, and woodpile on the other. The high-backed settle is a simply constructed Colonial wooden loveseat, built with a high back originally to keep off drafts. Under the seat is a storage chest. Next to the settle is an easy chair. Beside it, attached to the settle, is a small shelf just big enough to set a lamp on, for the chair and settle to share.

On the south wall next to the pantry is a 5×4-foot window with window seat, a bookcase, then another 5×4-foot window and window seat. There is storage under both window seats, and each of these has a lamp shelf attached to it.

In the southwest corner the stairway begins, curving along the west wall. The space under the upper part of the stairs, once they reach a height of 4½ feet, is used to accommodate a window and window seat. On the other side of this is a closet for coats, gloves, and boots just inside the front door.

On the other side of the front door is another pantry, this one for food only. Around the corner, on the north wall, is an auxiliary cookstove in front of a 6×4-foot window. (A family of ten can use the extra cooking potential.) Nearby are counters coming out from the wall, with open shelves beneath for storage of such things as dishpans, soap, garbage bucket, and water buckets. There are two stools at one end for two people to be working with food at once, and a cupboard opens out of the other side into the dining area for the dishes.

Beyond the counters, a 6×4-foot window gives light to the 6×4-foot table, and in the northeast corner is a small safe for special dishes. A 4×4-foot window gives additional eastern light from the east wall. The back door is located here also.

PLAN 12

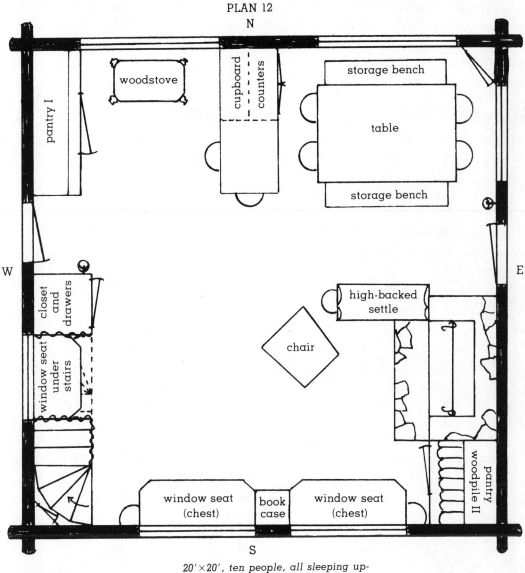

20'×20', ten people, all sleeping up-stairs.

PLAN 13

Plan 13 for ten is very similar to Plan 12. It, too, is 20-foot square, but some of the previous spaciousness has been partitioned off to give the parents a downstairs bedroom in case that is desired.

Beginning in the southeast corner is the bed, 5×8 feet, with shelf over-head, pegs on the wall for pajamas, and a 4×1½-foot closet with drawers. Above and beside the bed is a 4×4-foot east window. Adjacent to the bed's foot, but opening in the opposite direction, is the food pantry, facing the small stove with a 4×4-foot east window above it. The counters are beyond, going around the corner.

On the north wall beyond the counters is the table, with a 6×4-foot window. It would be possible to move the table just slightly nearer to the counters or to the stairway on the other side, and provide space for a back door, if one is desired.

PLAN 13

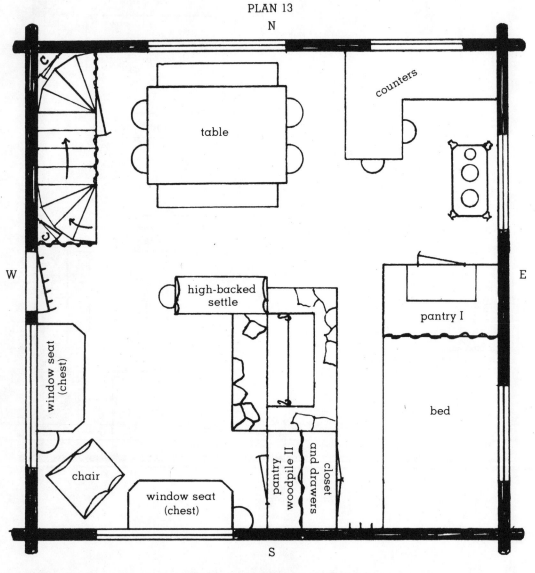

20'×20', ten people, parents sleeping downstairs.

The stairway is in the northwest corner, and under it is a closet for coats and boots. In the middle of the west wall is the front door, and next to it a 6×4-foot window with 4½-foot window seat beneath.

The second pantry, for pots and woodpile, comes out from the wall, and next to it is the fireplace and high-backed settle as before.

It would be easy to put in a door or hang a curtain across to cut off the bedroom if desired.

EXPANSIONS

There are two types of expansions, planned and unplanned. Planned expansions are foreseen from the beginning and carried out when convenient. Unplanned expansions suddenly burst upon you, when a family of six has to occupy a house suitable for only three, for example. When that happens, you have to add on, whether it's convenient or not—more often not. You can see the advantage of building the right size to start with, or adding on at a convenient time.

There are several types of additions, lean-tos, wings, and dormer windows. All of these can look as nice as the original building if you watch your step. The expanded horrors usually result when no effort has been made to keep the style of the addition consistent with that of the original building.

Dormers are usually thought of with regard to light, but they also provide sections of vertical wall against which things can be placed to better utilize space, so they can actually make your upstairs bigger as well as lighter.

The outside drawing of the 16-foot square with 60-degree Elizabethan roof, expanded version, has dormers shown on front and back. These are just one type of dormer, but one that is consistent with most styles. There are several other types, but the wrong choice can make the house look awful.

The difference between a wing and a lean-to is that a lean-to is a single-room one-story structure, with one-direction slanting roof, while a wing is the same height as the original house, with one or more rooms and the same roof pitch. A wing can be either added on at right angles, or as a continuation in the same direction. Lean-tos are quicker if you don't need the upstairs space provided by a wing.

Lean-tos for both original structure and later addition are very workable for planned expansion, since they are the quickest to build, and also offer pleasing combinations when expanded. The two expanded lean-to draw-

Fig. A

kitchen,
living,
sleeping

S

Fig. B

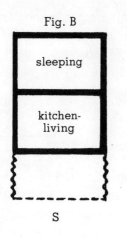

Fig. C.

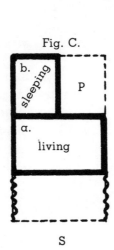

Fig. D

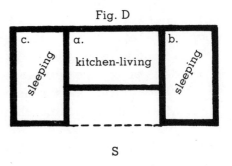

ings illustrate this. In each case, half was built at first, and half added later. Split-levels, as can be seen, adapt nicely to this idea.

When planning a structure to be expanded later, keep in mind the organizational possibilities offered by attaching the addition in different positions. Fig. B of the Expansion Shape Possibilities shows the original cabin, in this case a 10×16-foot, with a full-size addition on the north side, both for cool sleeping, and so that the kitchen-living area will not lose any of its valuable south, east, or west windows.

Fig. C shows an addition half the original size, again as a bedroom on the north, but this time there is a protected space for a cool north porch.

Fig. D would be good for a cold climate, since the additions enclose a sheltered south patio or porch area, and do not rob the original part of any south windows.

Fig. E

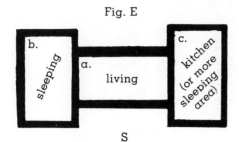

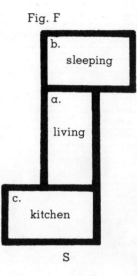

Fig. F

Fig. E offers a partially sheltered space on two sides, north and south, for a porch on one side and a patio on the other. A porch, by the way, also tends to make a north side warmer, since it offers the house some small protection from winds.

Fig. F is an appropriate shape for hot climates. It is designed to diffuse heat as much as possible, since a square or almost-square holds it in, and a sprawled-out shape loses it. In this case the kitchen is on the south side, and the sleeping quarters on the north. This may sound paradoxical, but the kitchen is going to be hot anyway, whereas the sleeping areas have to be as cool as they can, or you'll never sleep at all.

OUTSIDE DRAWINGS

The outside appearance of the cabin is going to be ruled to a large extent by the inside, but there is still a lot that can be done to make the exterior pleasing and practical. In looking through the drawings, which are on a ¼ inch = 1 foot scale, you will notice that the styles and roof pitches vary widely. There is considerable option here. Pitches, for example, are good for more than looks. Suppose you need the space of a full upstairs, but you don't like the idea of lifting logs high enough to build a second story, or

10'×10', gambrel roof, front view.

10'×10', gambrel roof, side view, cantilevered porch, porch built as part of original structure.

10′×16′, lean-to, front view, 30° roof.

10′×16′, lean-to, side view, 30° roof.

*10′×16′, lean-to, expanded version A,
"Down Home" style.*

maybe you just don't like the looks of two-story houses. On the other hand, you don't want to build a sprawling, ranch-style cabin because of the extremely long logs involved, and you don't want to have to expand later. A solution could be to build either a 60-degree roof or a gambrel and get a full upstairs and small attic above besides. Of course, like anything else, this idea has a disadvantage—it requires twice the roofing material of a two-story house with 30-degree roof.

On the other hand, if you are in a terrific hurry to get a cabin built before winter, the solution might be one of the tiny emergency cabins with a lean-to roof, very shallow pitch. This won't provide much room upstairs, but you may not need the space, and this takes the least roofing as well as being the quickest roof you can build.

An in-between roof, conventional type, with a pitch of 30–45 degrees, provides a compromise between the two extremes, with a fairly usable upstairs and not so much extra roofing needed.

Another consideration for how your house will look is the terrain you're

10'×16', lean-to, expanded version B, 30° roof, split-level.

*16'×16', 30° roof, Northwoods style,
cantilevered porch built in.*

building on. On sloping terrain the easiest plan is often to build a split-level. To many people's minds this is a fancy, exotic idea, but really it can be a way around a lot of work. It also provides a natural room divider, which can be exploited inside to make a very interesting and helpful effect.

Several of the drawings show a patterned effect over the windows. This is not expensive leaded glass, as you might think, but a simple framework of poles nailed on the outside of the window opening after the windows are in. Not only are these ornamental, often making all the difference in the cabin's looks, but also function as pest deterrents. And, of course, these are not structural, but can be added after the fact, at your leisure. They improve the inside appearance as well as the outside, and interfere surprisingly little with vision out the windows. But remember that there are any number of patterns, so be sure to pick one that is consistent with your house style.

A porch is also shown in several drawings. This is not necessary, of course, but it is certainly something to consider adding on. Presumably you are building a log cabin because you want to live closer to nature, and there

16′×16′, 60° roof, Elizabethan style.

*16′×16′, Elizabethan style, expanded
(dormers and porch added).*

16'×24', German medieval split-level, 45° roof, porch added later.

20'×20', gambrel with porch.

are plenty of times you'll like to sit out there and just look and listen. It's also a cool place to do sitting-down work in the summer if you build it on the north or east side.

A porch should be no less than 4 feet deep, and can be up to 8 feet on a large house. The deeper the porch, the less wet it will get in the rain, in case you're sitting out there or stacking wood there. The porch roof should be no less than 6 feet high on the low side, and higher is better. But don't get it over 8 feet, or it will rain in.

THINGS TO REMEMBER ABOUT LOG CABIN LIVING

If you're planning to live in your log cabin all the time, permanently, there are a few more things to keep in mind, which will have some effect on the design of your cabin. First, if you're planning to sleep upstairs, you will have to take precautions or you'll roast in the summer. Shade trees are priceless in keeping the sun's heat off the roof and consequently out of the upstairs. You should cut as many windows as the end walls will permit, and make supplemental air vents as well. These are easy. In any log cabin there is a gap under the eaves that ordinarily has to be chinked. For vents, just tack screen over instead of chinking, all along both sides, to produce an air flow. Finally, if your roof is thick, hewn slabs, it will already be fairly insulated, but if it is anything thinner, insulation will help. This can be conventional insulation, built-in if you have the money, or can be produced by boarding the inside of the attic beams to make an inner wall, so that air space insulates you.

If you're having trouble coming up with a feasibly small plan that will accommodate everything you want to put in your cabin, remember that beds do not have to be fixed. There are bunk beds, trundle beds, which store under a large bed in the daytime and are pulled out at night, and folding beds, which hang from a wall at night and fold out of the way in the daytime.

In the woods you always need storage for woodpile and tools. All our plans show some wood storage, but if it's not enough, remember you can put it under the cabin itself, and tools, too, especially with split-levels.

If you plan to raise a garden, you will need additional winter storage for your produce. Some vegetables will store well in the attic, if there is room, and for others you can easily dig a small root cellar under the floor after your cabin is built. This can be just a simple hole, 4 feet square and deep. Slant all the walls back a little at the top, and it need not be shored or stoned unless you wish. Make a wooden cover to help insulate it. You can reach it by means of a trap door in the floor.

Don't consider digging a full-size basement unless you stone or block it, since an unmortared cellar has a tendency to turn into a cistern, collecting all the surface water in the area.

When you really have time, there are other possibilities for food storage, too. A root cellar provides cool storage, but a spring house provides positive refrigeration, if you have the spring or stream needed. It is merely a small stone or at least stone-bottomed house, built right over a stream or down into a hill below a spring, so that water flows over the stone floor and out constantly. This continual movement of water cools the house both by conduction and by evaporation, and keeps food quite cold.

You can even make a freezer of sorts for use in the winter. All you need to start with is a large box, such as the window seats in many of the plans, or the space under a single bed closed in. Build a second box 6 inches smaller on all sides, top, and bottom than the first. Lay 6 inches of some sort of insulation on the floor in the larger box, then place the smaller box on it inside the larger box. Cram all the space between the two walls with insulation. For the lid, fill a cloth or plastic bag with insulation until it is 6 inches thick flattened out, and tack it to the underside of the lid. Next, cut several holes in the cabin wall clear through to the inside box. The holes should be perhaps 6×9 inches. Remove all the pieces, and replug the holes with solid blocks of wood fitted snugly, and which protrude enough on both ends to be removable from either outside the cabin or inside the box.

When the weather is near zero or colder, put the food you want frozen outside and let it freeze solid, at the same time opening all the outside holes so the box acquires the temperature of the outdoors. When the food is frozen, put it in the box and close up the holes. Keep them shut whenever the weather is much above zero, but open them whenever it's colder. In this way the food will keep frozen several months.

Baths and laundry always pose a problem initially. The pioneers took baths in a big washtub in front of the fire or stove, and this is still a good idea. Galvanized tubs shaped for the purpose sell for about $20, and can be hung up on a wall when not in use.

A bathhouse is also a handy idea, one which is still in use in rural areas. All it need be is a small building, perhaps 8-foot square, equipped with its own stove or fireplace for heating hot water and rocks. It can be built after the cabin is finished, or if you have built a temporary cabin and then moved into a permanent one, you can turn the old one into the bathhouse.

The principal advantage of having a bathhouse is that you can keep all washtubs there, rather than cluttering up the cabin with them, you heat all that water there and the steam harms nothing, and you can hang up your wet clothes there, regardless of weather. In winter you can also use it as a sugarhouse, for producing maple sugar: It can also be used as a sauna house, for taking immensely healthy sauna baths.

To do your laundry, place the clothes in a washtub, dishpan, or large kettle directly over the fire or on the stove with soap and cold water, and let them boil clean. (But only do this with cotton or linen, which can stand heat!) The boiling provides enough agitation to get them clean. This is what our grandmothers did, and it works. Wool and synthetics are a different story. Wool, especially, should never be placed near hot water or heat of any kind, but then it never gets too dirty anyway, and can always be washed out by hand.

Maybe you have had experiences with never being able to get enough hot water for a really comfortable and therapeutic bath. We certainly have. Well, in the woods you don't have that problem. It's true it would be a terrible bother to heat enough water in kettles for that kind of bath, but you don't do it that way. Instead, just fill the tub to the desired depth with cold water, and heat it in the tub by means of hot rocks heated in the fire or on top of or inside the stove. Heat a good many of these, taking care to use fairly hard rocks that are not from a creek bed, or they may explode or fall apart on you. When the rocks are red hot, carry them carefully with tongs and plunge them into the water, stepping back quickly to avoid possible steam burns. Enough of these rocks will heat it to exactly the temperature you want.

You can also improvise bathtubs in any number of ways, using old salvaged bathtubs, animal watering troughs, leather coracles, or a hand-built cement-mortared stone tub. Whatever you use, though, either plan to bail it out afterwards or provide a drain hole and plug, plus drainage of some kind, like a 3-foot deep pit full of gravel, underneath.

Until you have time to build a bathhouse, you can get by with sponge baths in the cabin itself, but a bathhouse is something you will certainly want to have when you can.

4

THE SITE AND THE FOUNDATION

CHOOSING A SITE

The right site is very important. It can make every step in building go like clockwork, or the wrong one can make it a nightmare, not only during building but for living in, too. It is seldom possible to find an ideal site these days. You probably already own the land you hope to build on, and your choice of site is limited to what is on it. Still, some study of the considerations involved will make it easier to choose the best site you can.

The most important consideration is water. Whether you plan to live on the site permanently or only occasionally, you'll need water to drink. What the source will be depends not only on what there is, but on what you consider acceptable. Some people would worry too much if they had to drink from a spring, stream, or lake, even if unpolluted. If you are one of these, remember that such water can be purified by boiling it or adding chemicals, if that proves to be the easiest water supply.

If there is no such source available, you can dig a well by hand or drive a hand pump. You can also dig a cistern. If you can afford it, and if the service is available, you can have a deep well drilled, if there is no shallow water. And, of course, there are always rainbarrels for an additional supply.

The next thing to look for is timber. Ideally, timber would be near the potential site, but not quite underfoot; otherwise, you will have to clear the site before building. Look around. Is there timber within a hundred yards and not downhill from the site? You can reasonably haul it that far, in the proper diameter and cut to size, without any assistance. If the timber is uphill from the site, you can stretch the distance a little, since it takes less effort to bring timber downhill.

You can even haul your logs uphill to the site without assistance, if absolutely necessary, provided they are no more than 25 yards away. Any farther and you become a work animal yourself. We know.

The opposite problem is having to clear your site. This may be the best course if the site that meets all the other qualifications is wooded. Just remember to cut off the trees near enough to the ground that you can put your floor in above them. If you plan to use a dirt floor for a while, they'll have to be cut off at ground level or below. This can be a very tedious process, so avoid it if you can.

Another thing you want is high ground, naturally well drained, but hopefully not steep mountainside. This is for ease of building and living, and also so your house will neither rot nor sink into the mire. You can build on stilts, but unless it is an absolute necessity, don't try it since it will certainly cause delay. If your ground is not extremely wet, however, you can build there if you are willing to take more trouble with the foundation, and afterwards with grading, ditching, and the like.

Level ground is a great advantage and makes for easier building, but it's not a necessity. It is far better to have a high, well-drained site that slopes than a level, boggy one, but if you can choose a site that has both advantages, don't ignore it.

Access can be a problem. It all depends on what your circumstances are and what you're willing to do. It can be by road, logging road, or waterway if you're prepared to bring everything in by boat. If an access route touches your property, make every effort to build near it, not only for such things as bringing in groceries and building materials but also for bringing in your possessions. Or be prepared to pack everything in by horse or mule, in a hand cart, or on your back. In Kentucky, we lived three-quarters of a mile from the nearest road, and had to pack 4,000 pounds on our backs, initially, through the woods and up a steep hill. It took four months. We also had to make a weekly seven-mile round trip to the grocery store, and each of us carried home about seventy pounds of groceries up that hill. This was one reason our cabin took so long to build. It can be done, but if this is your situation, be prepared and be hardy.

A southern exposure can make quite a difference. It's not an essential like wood and water, but in winter, windows on the south side give you the maximum of light and heat.

How much privacy is enough depends entirely on you. If you are building out "in the country," rather than in the wilds, remember the neighbors. You can plant screens of shrubs or evergreens later to help out with this, so don't worry too much about it.

Naturally, you should pay some attention to the view and the natural beauty of the site, provided it also meets as many of the other needs as possible. If the most suitable spot seems a little unimpressive, remember that the cabin will change the looks of it. Don't be misled by a wooded site, either, because it will look much different cleared. Choose mostly by facts, not looks. If you are considering a site, lay out a square or rectangle the size of your proposed cabin with poles or stakes and string, and stand inside and look around. This will help you imagine what it would be like to live there. If the technically perfect site is one that you know you could not live with, then by all means choose a more inconvenient, but beautiful, spot, if there is one. But remember you will have to pay the price.

Stone is a great asset for foundations, chimneys, homemade stoves, and walls. If there is stone on your property, you might still have to haul it some distance to the site if it isn't handy. So consider that, too.

And, last, if you plan to garden later, it will help to have a good garden site immediately adjacent to the cabin site, especially if you are far out in the wilds. There, the problem of wildlife eating your plants is much reduced by the garden's proximity to the house. In more settled country this is not as much of a problem.

THE FOUNDATION

Having designed your cabin and picked the site to build it on, you are now ready to begin, and the place to begin is with the foundation. The type of foundation you choose will be governed by the terrain and your circumstances. There are many kinds of foundations. Some are quick and easy but not durable, while others are time-consuming and difficult to build but last almost forever. Still others are reasonably quick and also fairly durable.

Very Quick Methods   The simplist foundation for level ground consists of laying the bottom logs halfway buried in the ground, with the second logs flush with the ground. This is probably the kind most familiar to anyone who thinks about log cabins, because many pioneers used it. However, the pioneers frequently did not plan to stay in one spot forever, or else planned to build a frame house later, and so were not concerned about durability. Then, too, they were usually building with large-diameter logs of very tough woods, so quick rot was not a problem. Today, you may occasionally still see one of these cabins standing intact. In these cases either the sill logs were of a very rot-resistant wood of large diameter, or the log next to the ground is not the original sill log but the second or even third one, which slowly settled as the previous one rotted out.

Such factors as soil type, climate, and roof overhang will affect the life expectancy of logs laid on the ground. Sandy soil is usually well drained, so water does not stand in contact with the sill very long. In dry climates there is not much rainfall to help rot the sill, while in a damp climate, like the Appalachians, sills tend to rot even on a foundation of rock. If you build a substantial overhang on the roof, it will prevent much of the rain from running down the walls and collecting around the sill, with the result of again lengthening the sill's life.

Where the ground sloped, the sill-in-dirt method was often varied slightly by propping one end of the sill up on rock or wood. This is a little better because ground that slopes is automatically better drained, and only one end of each sill is actually in the dirt; but that one end is still likely to rot and cause trouble in the not-too-distant future. If you are determined to use this method, at least use a rot-resistant wood or treat with a preservative.

There are other methods that are almost as quick, and are more durable and more repairable, should that need arise. The quickest foundation is made by simply putting one rock or block of wood at each corner and laying your sills on those. This will suffice for a small cabin, but for a larger one it is better to put a rock every 6 feet along the walls to prevent sagging. This method is just about as quick as the sills-in-dirt method, and much better.

If you use blocks of wood for this purpose, because you have no stones, bricks, or blocks, try to get seasoned chunks of a rot-resistant wood. If that's impossible, use green blocks of the same wood, or, as a last resort, whatever you have. It's much better, though, to look for good standing dead wood, and saw blocks off it. If you can treat the blocks with creosote or other preservative, so much the better, but have them tall enough so that no part of the sill is nearer than a foot to the ground. The higher they are, the longer they'll last; eighteen inches is even better.

If you have rock, and want to improve on this method slightly, use two rocks, one on top of each other, at each corner and between-point along the walls. The moisture that climbs up the lower rock by capillary action will be prevented by the second rock from reaching the sill log.

Better Foundations   A step beyond the previous category, but also a little more time-consuming, is to dig a pit at each corner and between-point, and sink one thick (12 inches or larger) post in it, going 3 feet deep and up to about 18 inches above ground, to support the cabin. An easier variation of this is a tight grouping of three postholes at each point, with a smaller post sunk in each, and the corners resting on all three together. To do this one, dig one of the holes and put a post in it before digging the next hole. Doing this with each of the postholes will prevent the holes from collapsing into each other or being impossible to dig due to the close proximity. Again, choose rot-resistant woods, or treat with a preservative, if possible.

The advantage of this foundation is that it goes down to below frostline to stabilize the cabin against movement of the ground, yet it can also be repaired later if it rots, by simply propping up the cabin temporarily with rocks or blocks while you dig out and replace the rotten supports.

If you have the materials, you can improve on this by digging the same posthole formations and filling them with gravel or small thrown stone.

(Don't dig pits in this case—it would take too much stone.) When you've dug them, enlarge the opening at the surface to make a hole 6 inches deep, encompassing the three postholes. Then fill the whole thing with stone, including the larger surface opening, and place your two rocks centered on each pile to build on. The wider surface opening will ensure the even transfer of weight to all three of the postholes equally. This foundation goes down to below frostline, and will never rot.

Another excellent filling material is cinders from an abandoned railroad bed. Even on tracks that are still in use, you may find places away from the tracks where there is a buildup of cinders resulting when the railroad company repeatedly dumped cinders, and some rolled off. But don't take them from the tracks themselves, or you'll be making trouble for the trains. They need those cinders to stabilize their tracks.

This type of foundation operates on the ballast system, the same system the railroad uses the cinders for. Any water that hits the cinders (or gravel or stone) is immediately drained, so it can't stand there and freeze when the weather turns cold. Any structure built on it is as stable, if not more so, than one with a solid mortared foundation.

There are other, more complicated methods, of course. You can support all the corners and midpoints on laid stone or cement block piers down to below frostline, or you can dig trenches all around the cabin's perimeter, fill with thrown stone, gravel, or cinders, then build an 18-inch laid foundation. You can dig and build an entire basement. You can even pour a concrete slab, footer, or basement.

All of these methods yield satisfactory results, but unless you are well off financially and are building a cabin as a recreational project, they are too impractical, requiring a great amount of time and money to achieve that result. For the homesteader, woodsman, or hermit, we do not recommend any of them.

Laying It Out   At this point you are ready to begin some of the actual work. You must keep in mind that log cabins are entirely different from conventional houses. Here, you're dealing with rough materials, while with a conventional house you have finished ones. So in laying your piers, posts, or rocks, realize that terms such as "level" are only roughly approximate, due to the uneven materials. Your eye alone, if it's halfway normal, can approximate "level" closely enough.

A few conventional building techniques do apply in building log cabins, and these are included here and there throughout this book, but with regard to foundations, they apply only in those cases where you're building a full basement or solid 3-foot-deep foundation. We are not including directions for that, since it is out of our province, and other excellent manuals have covered it.

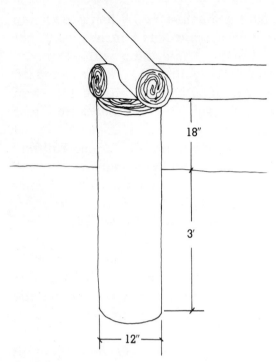

18"

3'

12"

A solid-post foundation.

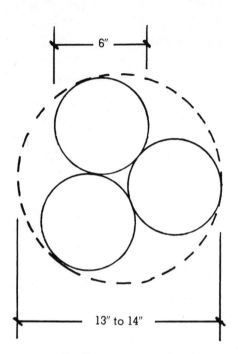

6"

13" to 14"

Small post-grouping foundation.

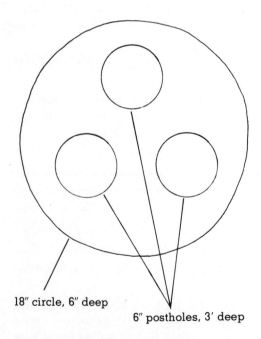

18" circle, 6" deep

6" postholes, 3' deep

Posthole formation for use with cinders, gravel, or thrown stone. Note that the postholes are spaced farther apart than for the small post-grouping foundation.

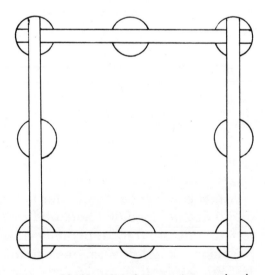

Marking foundation points on level ground.

The conventional stakes-and-string method of laying out a foundation is more trouble than it's worth for a log cabin. Instead, take your four sill logs, precut, premeasured, and marked about 1 foot from each end as described in the second half of Chapter 5. Notch two of them over the other two in the proper places, just as if you were starting to build, then pull them all into the exact position where you want the cabin. Check again to make sure all the marks are lined up, and each joint will then mark the center of a corner pit, block, or rock. Score the ground around the joint to mark the spot and mark between-points about every 6 feet along each wall as well. Then remove the logs, and go to work.

On sloping ground the procedure is slightly different. Get the sill logs ready as before, and drag them into position roughly. Here, though, because the ground slopes, it won't be possible to line up both the uphill and downhill ends as they will be when they're level, so be sure the downhill end is lined up exactly. Score the ground at the two downhill corners, and mark the between-points, then remove the logs. Start building those two corners, by whatever method you have chosen. While you're building, stop every now and then once you're well above ground level, and lay one of the side logs along the line of the future side wall, with its lower end on the pier you're building, to see if the pier looks high enough yet to make that log level.

When it looks level, remove the log, go round to the other downhill corner, and build that pier to about the same height. Try a log on it, and when it, too, looks level, put all four sills on again and mark the spots for the uphill foundation points. Build them as high above ground as desired, with or without pits underneath, then, after completing them, go down and build your downhill piers that same amount higher. Try the sills again. If the downhill end looks higher, and that is the end where you have the sills' butt ends, try reversing the logs. If the opposite is true, prop the downhill end up a little more. When it looks level, it is, as far as it needs to be.

After the four corners are done, you can leave the four sills on, and build the remaining points in under them with no trouble.

If your slope is steep, and you're building stone piers, take a shortcut and build with stone only for the first foot and a half above ground level. Then stand a sturdy post 12 inches or more thick firmly on top of that to go up the rest of the way. It's much easier than laying stone, and it will hold up just as well since it's up in the air. You will have to do some estimating to get the height right.

If you were using a post or posts to support each corner anyway, just cut them extra long so they can go all the way up on those downhill corners. Adjust the height of these by digging your holes deeper, blocking the post(s) higher, or in the event of a drastic change, sawing some off the post or adding an extra block—at the bottom of the holes for maximum strength.

Steep slopes are the reason for building split-levels. Instead of having to build such tall downhill piers, you build two separate foundations. Whatever you do, don't dig two flat places out of the hill (or even one) to build on. Prop it up, one level or two. It's much easier, faster, less damp, better drained, and more durable that way.

5
THE LOGS AND THE WALLS

WHAT KIND OF LOGS?

The cutting of the logs should be done as soon as you have designed the cabin you want and picked the site for it. For the walls themselves, you will need about fifty to sixty logs, averaging 6 to 7 inches in diameter at the halfway point between the large and small ends. You can make the diameter at the base up to 9 inches in a severely tapering log.

The pioneers in various areas used much larger logs, ranging from 10-inch oak on up to 2½-foot tulip, but if you are building a cabin by yourself, without a lot of animal or mechanical assistance, forget those large logs. You really don't need them, anyway. If you built a cabin out of 4-inch logs (not a bad idea for a tiny, emergency cabin) your walls would still be stronger than those of a modern balloon-frame house.

The length of the logs should be the inside dimension plus 2 feet. Cutting them to exact size right from the start will make for easier building, and helps in laying out the foundation. We had a chain saw, and thought it would be simple to cut them roughly at first, then go around after we were done building and trim all the log ends to size. This actually made building harder, and it also took a good deal more time to trim those ends later than we had expected.

What kind of wood should you use? You need not use one kind solely. Whatever kinds abound on your property are probably the ones to choose, selecting those that are reasonably straight and sound. Some woods are more desirable than others, of course, so here are a few guidelines in case you have a choice.

In the Appalachian region, tulip trees (commercial yellow poplar) are usually plentiful and are excellent, being tall and straight, light and strong, soft, and easily felled and notched. Another softwood abundant in that region is shortleaf pine, or Southern yellow pine. (Local names will differ; in our area tulip was just called poplar, and shortleaf pine was black pine.)

Shortleaf pine, growing quite straight, is also used for commercial lumber, and, when dry, is light and strong. Like other softwoods, it works easily, although, because of the resin, it is more difficult to saw than to chop. It is also very heavy when green, and more difficult to lift and drag than tulip.

You can choose from many of the finest hardwoods in that forest region, including hickory, oak, maple, locust (black), and beech. Hardwoods have a way of lasting forever, but are also much more difficult to work and will take longer to build. Given the above choices, pick oak, preferably one of the white oak family. It works much more easily than the others, but watch out for its weight. Like the other hardwoods, it is very heavy when green.

The North Woods, New England, and the Rocky Mountains have a forest region quite different from that of the Appalachians. There, conifers and a few sturdy broadleaf hardwood and softwood species predominate. In those areas, cabins are usually built of pines or spruces. Other conifers, too, are used, and tamarack, or larch, is considered excellent when it is found in sufficient quantity, usually in low, swampy areas.

Quaking and bigtooth aspens (frequently called popple) are also used, though they do not hold up as long. If it is necessary to use them, and you cannot obtain sill logs of a better wood, you might use slightly thicker ones near the ground, or paint them when seasoned with creosote or other preservative. Birch is another good wood for cabins, if you can get enough of it. Yellow birch is a hardwood, more durable but also heavier and harder to work. White birch is softer, less durable, but easier to work with and drag. It is always a good idea to ask the locals what they have used, or maybe what their parents or grandparents used, and why. Remember that local

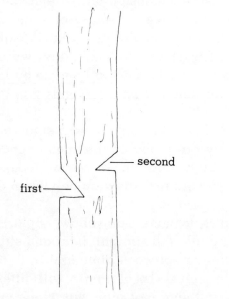

Notching a tree to fell it.

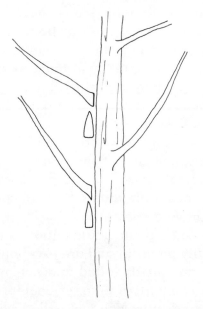

The right way to trim off branches.

names can be confusing, though, and make sure of proper identification.

Since sill logs are closest to the ground, and consequently subject to the most damp and possibility of rot, you might wish to choose a special type of wood for them, if available. There are several kinds of wood known for their resistance to rot on or near the ground, among them black locust, which is famous for it, and tamarack, its northern and western counterpart. Tulip poplar, too, has been widely used for sills, and often holds up for a very long time. In general, water woods, or those that grow in damp or boggy locations, are a fairly good bet for sills, though some are not so good. Black walnut, eastern red cedar, and northern white cedar are good ones, but don't indiscriminately try some of the others.

As mentioned above, if you can't obtain any of the good sill woods, a coat of creosote or the like will help to preserve what you have, and if you can't afford that, just use thicker logs, perhaps 10 inches through.

CUTTING THE TREES

Whatever tool you are using, the best height at which to cut is from 2 to 3 feet above the ground. This may seem to waste valuable wood, but it will save work and not waste, either, for the following reasons: first, the base of a tree has more water in it than any other part, and is also nearest the ground. This combination results in the wood's being tougher and twistier than the rest of the tree, and, frequently, in the base being rotten. This means it is going to be much more difficult to cut, and is likely to be rotten when it is cut, and thus no good for building. Second, it is much more uncomfortable for a person to bend over and cut near the ground than it is for him to cut higher up, thus requiring more energy and time. It is also much more likely that he may hit the dirt with the cutting edge of his tool, which would require more time and energy to correct by sharpening. So avoid difficulties by cutting at the right height.

In choosing your trees, try to select those that don't seem to be leaning in any particular direction. If you have to use some that are leaning, see the procedures given a little later in this chapter. For an ordinary tree, though, first decide which way you want it to fall, then cut a notch out of the side of the tree facing that direction. The notch should be as high from the bottom edge to the top as the tree is thick, and the narrow point of the notch should go all the way to the tree's center. The notch will tend to immediately transfer most of the tree's weight in the direction you want the tree to fall, and can be made with either axe or saw. If the tree should fall before you are ready, it will fall approximately where you want it to anyway.

After making that notch, go around to the opposite side and cut a smaller notch, higher up, so that the narrow points of both notches line up down the center, the second above the first. By the time you have done this, your tree should already be falling. If it trembles in the balance, as sometimes happens, you can easily give it a push. But be sure to stand well away from the butt and off to the side, when it begins to fall, for a tree will frequently jump backwards and sideways off the stump, sometimes injuring or killing the unwary chopper.

If you are using a saw, you may find it being pinched sometimes by the tree's weight. Most trees will fall without pinching, but a leaning tree is almost sure to pinch. When the saw is pinched, you can liberate it, and probably fell the tree at the same time, by the use of a wedge and sledge hammer or maul. Beat the wedge into the cut you were working on, being careful not to hit your saw blade with it, and the tree will probably begin to tip. When it does, push it as well, to get the tree moving quickly, and pull your saw out and away very fast because the butt end can demolish the saw if it is still on the stump when the tree hits the ground. If wedging doesn't tip the tree, your saw will at least be free to continue sawing until the tree does fall. This works especially well with a Swedish saw.

FELLING LEANING TREES

If you have to make use of trees that lean, you will probably need to know some techniques. Of course, if a tree leans in a direction where it is all right to let it fall, there is no problem. Felling will be easy, with one exception: do not cut the first notch into the side toward which it leans. Just notch or saw a straight line into the opposite side, and it will fall with no trouble.

If you can't allow it to fall in the direction it wants to, then use one or more of the following procedures:

Before beginning to cut, tie a strong rope (half-inch nylon or polypropylene) to the trunk or a strong branch of the tree, some 10 to 15 feet up. Make the other end fast to another tree on the side opposite to the way it leans. Don't pull it taut, but don't leave too much slack either. Then make your first notch at right angles to the way it leans, and the second notch opposite it. When it starts to lean, clear out! That tree is going to do a lot of moving. It will try to fall the way it was leaning, but being prevented from doing that by the rope, it will pivot on its trunk and fall approximately at right angles to the rope. In the meantime, the trunk is more likely than usual to hurt you in the process, so be very careful.

Another aid is a springy green pole 3 to 4 inches thick, with a crotch at the top. This is wedged under the trunk of the tree on the leaning side, and dug into the ground. Then, when the tree begins to fall, the springiness of the pole will tend to deflect it to the side instead of the direction it wanted to go. Again, remember to put your notches at right angles to the lean.

A third plan involves a partner standing on the side opposite to the lean, holding a rope attached as described earlier, ready to pull the tree in the desired direction when it starts to fall.

Whichever method you use, don't try to fell a tree opposite to the way it leans, or you'll run into trouble. Be content with felling it to one side, which is much easier and surer.

TRIMMING MEASURING

Once a tree is down you have to trim off the branches and cut it into the right lengths. Don't fell several trees at once, then try to trim and measure them all. It's much more troublesome. Do each one as you fell it.

Use an axe for trimming unless you have a chain saw. To trim, stand on one side of the fallen trunk and work on the other; that way the trunk is between you and any misstrokes. Swing the axe parallel to the trunk, as close to it as possible, and cut from the lower side of each branch (as the tree stood) to the upper, right where the branch joins the trunk. This removes the branch cleanly, while cutting the other direction will tend to split the trunk.

After trimming, take a measuring tape or premeasured string or pole and measure off your lengths. Do a good job of measuring because this will save trouble later. Try to get more than one length out of each tree if you can, so you won't have to fell any more trees than necessary. Then take them, length by length, back to the site.

DRAGGING

You may not have to drag the trees very far, if they were cut near the site. Even if you do, you should be able to move them easily enough if you use the size recommended and they are not terribly long.

There are techniques to help. One of these is a pole for rolling. This is just a green pole, branches removed, about 10 feet long. Simply insert the larger end as far beneath the log to be moved as you can, then lift up the other end of the pole, and let the log roll forward off it. If moving uphill, be sure to stop the log before it can roll backwards again.

Another method of moving it is to lift one end of a log, carry it forward as far as you can, and let it down. Then go back and do the same thing with the other end, and so on, alternating. This is a good method for moving logs uphill.

For taking them over level ground, you can manually roll them along pretty easily. You can also frequently pick up a log and carry it, depending on its weight, your strength, and the terrain. This is the simplest way if you can do it. But where there are a lot of deadfalls or brush due to previous felling of trees, it is easiest to roll logs right over the obstacles, instead of carrying them.

BARKING

Once you get the logs to the site, you should bark them if you plan on doing so. The reason you waited until now is that the bark gives traction for your hands, and makes moving them much easier. It is not absolutely necessary to remove the bark before building. If you are in a desperate hurry for shelter, avoid it. Otherwise, take the time to do it.

Bark is pretty and woodsy, but there is no known preservative for it. If you leave it on, it will provide an excellent home for woodworms and insects of all types, and will serve as a sponge to keep damp next to your wood, which makes it rot faster. It will also make the inside of the cabin feel damper and clammier. And, after all this, in six months or a year it will fall off anyway, in little dribs and drabs, falling in your food and other inconvenient places. So take it off at the beginning if you possibly can.

The easiest time to bark logs is in the spring. The sap is up and the bark is removed with comparative ease, depending upon the kind of tree. In that season, the bark of such trees as birch and tulip will come off in a big sheet if you make a slit the whole length of the log with an axe, pry under both edges gently all along with a spud, then keep prying gradually deeper and deeper until you have loosened it all. Where it sticks around knots (places where branches were attached), pound at the knot with a wooden maul to loosen it, then try prying again.

Some trees, even in spring, have to have their bark hacked off bit by bit with an axe or removed in narrow strips with a drawknife. And this is true even of tulip and birch at some times of year. Just keep at it, though, and it won't take forever.

The best way is to bark each log as you get it to the site, rather than waiting and doing them all at once. Unless you have help, that can be very tedious, but one log at a time isn't so bad.

SEASONING

You are supposed to season your logs at least six months (a year is even better) after they are cut before building with them. As logs dry out, they shrink because of losing all that water, and finally assume approximately their permanent sizes. Seasoned logs are lighter to handle, too, and your chinking will not tend to fall out as easily as if the logs were shrinking on the wall.

Building with green logs means that, when they have shrunk, the cracks between logs that were 2 inches high may be almost 3 inches. So, of course, the chinking that filled 2-inch cracks won't fill 3-inch ones, and you'll have to replace it. But if you are chinking with mud, you'll have to re-do that every year anyway. Even if you plan to use clay or cement, it's better to use mud the first year and replace it later, since even seasoned logs will shrink some more when one side of them is exposed to the heat of a stove or fireplace. So you don't really lose anything by building with green logs.

Still, if you can season your logs for even six months, by all means do so, since it makes lighter logs to lift. For six-month seasoning, it's best to cut them in the fall, when there is least sap in them to begin with, and come back to build in the spring, which is the best time to begin building anyway.

Logs will season better if you bark them first, but if you don't have the time, remove two strips of bark running the log's whole length, on opposite sides. This can be done with a hatchet, small axe, or drawknife, and won't take long, but it will cause the checks (cracks which all logs develop during seasoning) to occur along those two lines, where the water will be breathed out most easily, rather than being equally distributed. The log will be stronger this way. Then, when you build, place them on the walls with the checks on top and bottom where they will be best protected from moisture:

There are different methods of seasoning, but the principal way is to arrange the logs up off the ground so that they are exposed to air on all sides.

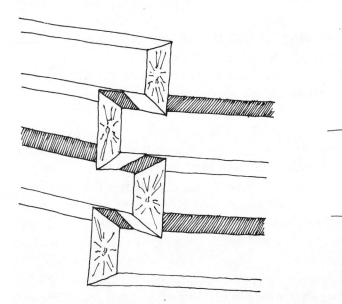

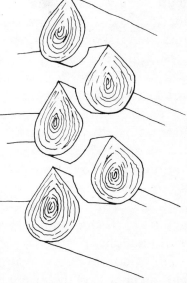

Square dovetail notch.

Round dovetail notch.

They do not have to be under cover, since, up in the air, they will quickly dry after getting wet. You can also season them by laying them on brush, if you have lots, or stacking them in a crisscross pile. You can even season them on the stump before you cut them down, by the ancient Indian method of girdling.

To girdle a tree, take a hatchet or small axe and remove a ring of bark about 2 feet wide all around the tree—and that is all. This kills the tree, and all the sap will dry up. Then you can come back in six months or a year, and cut your trees already seasoned. This is not quite as simple as it sounds, though. The Indians chose this method because they were going to burn the tree down, rather than cut it, since they had only stone axes, and seasoned wood burns more easily than green. But seasoned wood is much harder to chop than green, although it will saw more easily. Don't do it, then, if you plan to cut with an axe.

THE WALLS

Now you are finally ready to start laying up the logs. The first thing that will probably occur to you is that walls should be square, plumb, and level. This idea has grown out of modern house-construction techniques. But log cabins are different, and the same rules don't apply. What can be done with finished materials is vastly different from what you can do with rough ones, like logs. No matter how much time and effort you spend, you cannot possibly make a log cabin more than approximately meet these standards.

But you shouldn't want to, anyway. Log cabins are rough, and much of their beauty lies in their very imperfections. You could pay absolutely no attention to the matter while building, and still end up with a cabin almost indistinguishable from one that you endlessly slaved over.

Still, in case such matters worry you, here are some methods that will let you get as close to those objectives mentioned as you can without a great waste of time and energy.

Keeping fairly level is easy. All you have to do is alternate butt ends of logs with narrow ends. For example, if you put the butt end of the bottom log on a particular side on your right, you will put the butt end of the second log on that side to your left, and so on. After a log is notched into position, if one end sticks up more than an inch or so above the other end, notch the high end a little deeper so it will sit down lower. You can also check the middle of the log with a level, but it's not at all necessary. Your eye will do well enough.

On a lean-to cabin, you do not want your walls level, so just put all the butt ends one on top of another to achieve the effect of one tall side and one short. Spike each joint in place after fitting it to assure stability, since this construction will tend to move if it can.

Keeping your walls square and plumb can be done in various ways, most of them harassing, but we found a method that accomplishes both these things at once and is not too troublesome, either. It begins when you cut your logs to exact size, inside dimension plus 2 feet, as described earlier. This allows one extra foot at each end for notching and overhang. (After notching, there will be no more than 6 inches of overhang, which is better than the longer ones often found, since it will not stick out as far to get wet, and so lasts longer.)

Before notching each log, take a measuring tape and remeasure the log to find its exact length. If it is what it should be, measure in one foot from each end, and make a mark with your axe. If the length was an inch or so too long, add that distance to the one foot at one end, and measure and mark 13 inches (or whatever it comes to) from the end instead. If it was an inch too short, measure in only 11 inches at one end, and mark there. The main thing is to have the exact inside dimension of your cabin between those two marks.

Next, put the log up on the wall, positioning it so that the mark at each end lines up above the thickest part of the log it will be notched over. When you roll the log over to notch, the marks should be directly on top. Your notch should begin at that mark and go toward the end of the log, the width being that of the log it will fit over. That way each inside wall will be the correct size, and the whole cabin will consequently be square and plumb. However, the more crooked the logs, the more juggling you'll have to do and the less these rules will apply.

FLOOR JOISTS

If your ground is extremely level, and you are planning on a dirt or stone floor, you won't have the problem of laying floor joists. Otherwise, though, the time to lay them is right after the sills are laid. The reason for doing it so early is that you need to know where floor level is in order to calculate how high to build your walls and at what height to put your windows. Methods for doing this are given in Chapter 7 in the section on floors. Another advantage to this is that you can temporarily floor in portions of it very roughly with logs to stand on while working.

Remember to consider roof overhang in relation to the height of your doors. Your main door will swing inward, but if you should want to add a storm or screen door later, a low roof overhang might prevent it from swinging open. If you discover this to be the situation, you can always cut a chunk out of the roof above the door, but this is not really desirable because of less rain protection. Prevention is better than cure, and the easy way to avoid this situation is to build the cabin walls plenty high to begin with.

NOTCHING

There are quite a few different kinds of notches, some extremely simple, others complicated. The square dovetail notch and the round dovetail notch are beautiful but difficult, requiring much time, and, because of the exposed upper surfaces of wood involved, are not as durable as they might be. The upright saddle notch and double saddle notch are simple to make, but have the same trouble with exposed upper wood surfaces.

Consequently, there is really only one type of notch worth describing for the practical-minded, the inverted saddle notch, which is the best for all purposes even if you don't want to use an axe. It is very simple to make and holds the cabin together firmly. It also sheds water well, since no exposed wood surface is turned upward to catch rain.

To make it, put your log into position on the wall, lining it up carefully as described earlier. Then carefully roll it over away from you as you are sitting or standing at the corner of the walls. Check to make sure your marks still line up, and wedge it with chips to keep it from rolling while you chop. Then chop a rounded notch at each end in what will be the finished log's underside, beginning at the mark and continuing out toward the end. Getting the notch to fit over the log beneath is easy; it is done by eye. Begin at the mark and make the notch as wide as the log beneath is thick. When you put it in place, it will fit closely enough. You don't need anything approaching a perfect fit, but you may be surprised at how often you get just that without worrying about it.

The notch should be only one-third the log's thickness in depth, or about 2 inches deep with a 6-inch log. This will leave a gap of equal depth between each log and the next. It is possible to fit the logs closer by making the notches deeper, but this is not desirable. In the first place, those cracks constitute a ladder up the walls, very handy for putting on the upper logs and the roof. And second, they make chinking easier.

We thought it would be much cleaner to fit our logs so closely that there would be no cracks at all and we wouldn't have to chink. But we found that we still had to chink, to keep out bugs in summer and wind in winter. Since you are going to have to chink, it is better to leave big cracks that you can push your chinking into. Another advantage of large cracks is that it takes fewer logs to get to the top of the walls; therefore less felling, dragging, barking, and notching.

In case you are convinced that you cannot successfully use a small axe for notching, it is possible to make an inverted saddle notch with a saw, chisel, and mallet. All the measuring, marking, and other procedures remain the same, right up to the time of notching itself.

To notch, make two cuts with your saw, one at your mark, one as far from it toward the end as the log it will fit over is thick. You could make these cuts straight down, but it's better to slant them in toward each other. That will make for a tighter fit in the finished notch. The cuts should go no more than one-third deep, as before. When they are made, lay aside your saw, taking care to place it safely where it cannot cause any trouble. Place your chisel blade horizontally along the imaginary line connecting the bases of both cuts, and hit the chisel butt sharply with the mallet. Move the blade along that line, hitting repeatedly until the whole middle section starts to lift up. Roll the log toward you a little, so that the opposite side of the notch is within your working reach, and do the same on that side, until the whole chip splits out. This can also be done by hitting sideways with your axe. Then that notch is done. You'll find that there are corners you can see through, but this makes no difference, since you'll be chinking it anyway.

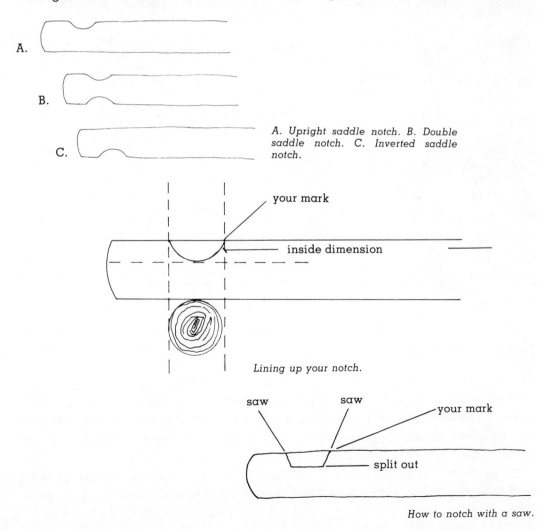

A. Upright saddle notch. B. Double saddle notch. C. Inverted saddle notch.

Lining up your notch.

How to notch with a saw.

NO-NOTCH METHOD

There are other methods of making log walls besides notching them to-gether horizontally. Most of them are harder than notching, but one that is fairly quick begins with driving two posts as tall as your proposed walls into the ground at each corner, at an angle to the walls. Slant the tops of each pair in toward each other slightly, then just lay the logs between them as usual, with the logs being held in place by the posts. Slanting the posts as described will make a tighter fit because they will be slightly sprung when a thicker log forces them outwards. This method will go very quickly, leaving large gaps, but chinking is easy.

When you get up to the top of the walls, nail or peg the tops of each pair of posts together with braces, and make sure the roof overhangs the corners. This structure could be used for a temporary dwelling, an animal pen (with-out roof), or shed for tools; since it is not as durable as a building on some sort of foundation, we would not recommend it for a permanent home.

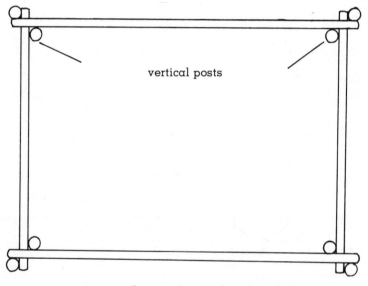

vertical posts

A no-notch method.

LAYING THE LOGS

If your cabin is square, it doesn't matter which two logs you lay first. Oth-erwise, lay the sills on the long sides first, so the foundation posts or blocks on those sides, where there will have to be more of them, will not have to be build any higher than necessary.

Some of your logs will be thicker than others no matter how hard you try to get them all the same size. Unless you have special logs for your sills, of rot-resistant wood, pick the largest of each length for that purpose. Even if you have special sills, use your thicker logs right above that. Being thicker, they will be more durable in proximity to the ground, and, besides, you might just as well not lift the thicker logs any higher than you have to.

When the walls become too high for notching from the ground, simply climb up on the walls and do it. The easiest way to do this is to straddle the corner, using the ladderlike openings to stabilize your position while notching. The position can vary depending on what's comfortable for you.

The small axe recommended in Chapter 2 is very maneuverable and works wonders. We found it such a handy instrument that we did all of our notching with it.

BUILDING ON STEEP GROUND

An aid to building on steep ground that can also be enjoyed later is a simple log porch-platform, built at the same time the sills are laid. First cut the two side sill logs (those that run from the uphill end to the downhill end) some 6 feet longer than the rest, and let the extra length extend beyond the downhill foundation piers or posts. If you have one or two midpoint foundation supports along the uphill and downhill walls, run one or two more long logs across them, too, parallel to the long sills. Then fit your other two sills, notching them over the in-between logs as well as the lower sills.

After that, take ten to fifteen logs 4 to 6 inches thick, and long enough to span the width of those log extensions, and notch each one into position to form a rough porch floor. If extra support is needed, you can run diagonal braces from the downhill edge of the porch, at the end of the supporting sills, down to the bases of the foundation posts. The flooring shouldn't even need nailing or pegging, and will make a working platform now, once you make a rough ladder up to it, and a pleasing porch later.

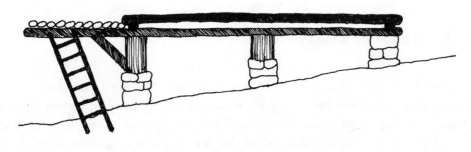

A porch-platform for help in building on steep ground.

SPLIT-LEVELS

On a split-level cabin, build the lower section first, with four walls, just as if it were the entire cabin, until it is high enough to put the first long log on. Remember, that first long log is not near the ground on the lower section, but it is the sill log of the upper section, so, if you have rot-resistant wood, this is the place to put it. From then on, just continue building with long and short logs.

If you are adding a lean-to expansion to an already-existing lean-to cabin on level ground, you need to build only three walls. The two outside corners of the addition should be notched as usual, with all the small ends at the outer corners and all the butt ends abutting against the original cabin's high wall. Each butt end should be trimmed to a rough point, and the point fitted into a corresponding gap in the original wall. For example, the sill log of the new part should fit into the gap directly above the sill log of the old part, the second new log into the next gap, and so on. Toenail each point with one 16-penny nail to stabilize it.

If you're adding the same sort of lean-to expansion to a lean-to cabin on sloping ground, make it a split-level and build three-and-a-half walls. Depending on whether your addition is uphill or downhill of the original portion, that half wall will be below or above the old cabin. If below, just build that fourth wall up until there's a gap in the original wall to use for the next log of the addition. If above, begin building the fourth wall when you're above the last gap in the old cabin's high wall.

Note: the drawing of a split-level lean-to in Chapter 3 is a different kind of cabin from what we have just been talking about. That one is of ordinary log cabin construction with frame endwalls, rather than actual lean-to construction, even though it has a lean-to type roof. We haven't included instructions for this type because it is not one of the most practical ones. If you want to build it, you can figure it out easily enough. If in any doubt, though, just skip it. But don't try to use that drawing as a guide for construction, except for the bottom parts of it, unless it is the exact type you plan to build.

TECHNIQUES FOR RAISING LOGS

The quickest and easiest way to get logs onto the wall is to lift them one end at a time, provided you have the strength. Most people, if they are using the right size logs and building a small enough cabin, should be able to do this. If it becomes too difficult after the walls pass a certain height, there are a couple of methods to help out.

One method involves the use of a hand-built ladder made out of poles. The ladder needs to be long enough so that even at the top of your walls it will not stand at an angle of more than 45 degrees because that would make lifting harder. A 14-foot ladder should do for an 8-foot wall plus 18-inch foundation height. The thickness, which should vary with the length, should be about 4 inches for both verticals and rungs for the length given, assuming green wood. To make the ladder, you need two long poles for the verticals and enough rungs 2 feet long to be distributed at 1-foot intervals all along the ladder. Lay the verticals out parallel on the ground, and chop shallow notches at carefully measured 1-foot spacing. Make sure each notch exactly lines up with its counterpart on the other vertical. Then lay each rung across a pair of notches, and nail it very firmly. You could, of course, attach the rungs with pegs, but it would take much longer.

The ladder's rungs, which stick up beyond the sides when the ladder is standing in position, are like steps. Stand the ladder against your highest log so far and centered on that wall, making sure the ladder's top doesn't stick up beyond that log more than an inch or so. Then stand at the bottom and lift the center of your next log onto the bottom rung, both its ends in the air. The unusual width of the ladder will help to minimize seesawing of the ends while you are lifting. Then just move the log along one step at a time, climbing the ladder yourself behind the log. This is a good position for lifting.

The ladder's angle will become steeper with each successive log, and it will have to be moved around the cabin, too, for use on the other walls. If frequently moving the ladder is a drain on you, you can build four such ladders with little trouble and leave one at each wall.

Another method does away with friction by using the principle of the wheel and brakes. First, you will need two skids for each wall. The length and thickness of these should follow the same rules as for the ladder above, and each should have one side hewn off shallowly to form a flat surface. The flat surfaces should then be shallowly notched at an angle, 1 to 1½ inches deep at the deep ends, at 2-foot intervals all along. Then place two along each wall, at roughly the one-third and two-thirds points along the wall, and running to the highest log as described for the ladder method.

Next you need two 35-foot ropes. These should be tied to the highest log on the side you're working on, one rope about a foot in from each corner. Tie them firmly, with pressure knots. Climb down and roll your next log into po-

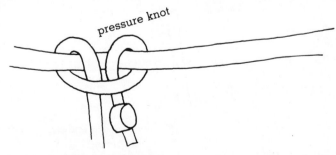

Pressure knot.

sition at the base of the two skids. Now, lift the log, one end at a time, into the first notch, to get it started, then pass the ropes under the log, around and over it, and carry the two ends back up. There should be several feet to spare at the ends for you to hold on to, and these should be knotted at 1-foot intervals.

Winding one of the ropes around the log loosely for safekeeping, go down to the other corner and sit down not on the wall you're working on but on the wall at right angles to it, as near as possible to the corner. Face the wall you're working on, and brace yourself very firmly with your legs, putting your feet in the cracks beneath you so that you can lean way forward and way back without losing your hold or your balance. Then lean forward, take a good hold on the rope, and pull, keeping a good watch on what the log is doing. It will take surprisingly little strength to move the log's end up to the next notch. While you're there, move it up one more notch, then wind the rope's end securely around the log to hold, and go do the same thing at the other corner. Don't try moving an end more than two notches before raising the other end equally, or the log will start to slip.

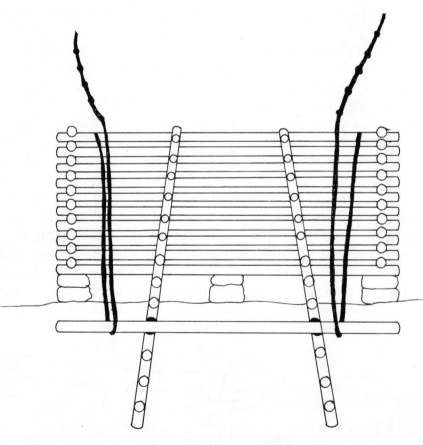

The notched-skid-and-ropes method
of raising logs.

At worst, it should take no more than half an hour to get a log up. At that rate, even with a four-hour workday, you'll have your walls up in about a week from the time you begin them. And that's pretty good.

On steep or sloping ground, you can build the porch-platform described earlier to aid in getting the logs onto the walls. If you prefer, you can simply put the logs intended for the downhill wall or either side onto the uphill wall, just as if they were to go there. Then either roll them down to the downhill wall or pivot them onto one of the sides.

WINDOW AND DOOR HOLES

The design for your cabin should have included the width, height, and location of the windows and doors. There are two basic methods for obtaining the holes for them, the first being to build them in, and the second to cut them out later on. With either method, you have to find by measuring where a window should be on a certain wall. With the first method, the time to do this is when the walls are as high or a little higher above the floor level than the windowsills should be. With the second, do it when the walls are a little higher than the windowtops should be.

Supposing that a window should be 4 feet in from a corner, measure that distance horizontally from the corner, along your floor joists on the inside if you have them and along the inside floor if not. Mark the floor joist or sill log at that point, then take a plumb bob and hang it on the wall a little higher than the windowsill should be, so that the string exactly passes through the mark you just made. Nail it there or have someone hold it steady while you measure the windowsill height up along it, and mark that point. That gives you the near lower corner of the window, and from there it will be easy to measure sideways and upwards to get the other corners. The easiest way to do this is to use chalked string.

Whichever method you are using, you need a larger hole than you want your finished window to be because it has to accommodate the board frame as well as the window itself.

If you prefer to saw the windows out, it is best to do it when the walls are just about as high as the windowtops are supposed to be. Check with plumb bob and measuring tape when you think you are getting close to the right height. If you find upon measuring that the windowtop is going to come partway into a log, move the window hole up or down, whichever is easier, so that the top occurs at a crack. A window's height is not usually so particular that a few inches up or down will ruin it. You do this because you want to be able to begin sawing downward right through the highest log you have yet laid, making it easier to start the saw. If you moved the window down,

measuring points

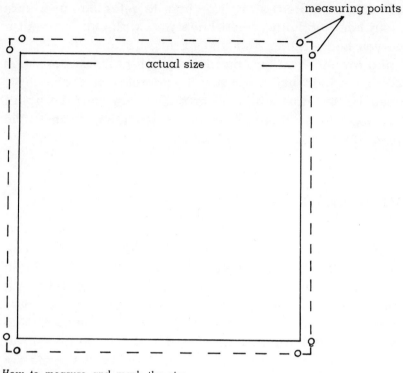

actual size

How to measure and mark the size
hole to accommodate the window
and frame.

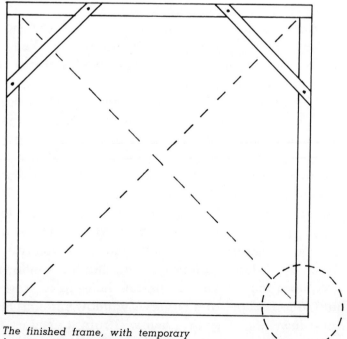

The finished frame, with temporary
braces nailed on. The circled area
shows the simple joint. The dotted diagonal measurements are equal, so
the frame is square.

and find you now have an extra log on top, just remove it temporarily and proceed with your sawing operation, and when that has been finished, simply replace the log again.

The pioneers usually built their walls entirely up to the top and put the roof on before cutting out the windows. This was for several reasons. First, they often traded labor to get help building the walls, so they wanted to get done with them quickly, rather than stop to do something they didn't need any help with. Then, too, they rarely had more than a couple of windows, and small ones at that, so it wasn't that much trouble to do it later. And third, the roof was considered all-important, and the windows mere luxuries. The pioneers took care of first things first.

After you get done marking out the enlarged dimensions of the hole, you'll need guidelines to saw along. You can make them either with a chalked-string line connecting your corner points or by nailing up two boards. The second method has the advantage that the nails you put through the boards into each log will hold those logs in place so they can't collapse. If you mark with a chalked string, you'll have to solve that problem by inserting small chunks of wood into the cracks. Or you can use the rope-and-poles method described in the windows section of Chapter 7. When your guidelines are finished, go ahead and saw out the hole, and get out of the way of the falling log section.

If you prefer to build in the board frames as you go, begin by measuring as before to find the two lower corners, this time when the walls are the height or a little higher than the windowsill should be. With this method you dispense with the upper corners. Mark the lower corner points, then enlarge them in both directions as before to allow for the thickness of the wooden frame. If you stopped building at the right height, your marks should all be somewhere along the highest log you've laid. If they're somewhere in the middle of it, you'll have to chop or make saw cuts down to that level, and split out the portion of log above it. If the marks fell right at a crack, of course, simply attach the frame in position there, once it is finished.

The procedure for building the frame is the same whether you put them in and build around them or cut the holes out later. The frame is built on the ground, then fitted in the space. (The one exception to this is if you have no nails and are using hewn slabs for the frame. In this case, cut the holes out according to the second method, and peg your slabs directly to the sides, top, and bottom of the hole.)

You can make the frames out of hewn slabs, boards, two-by-four's, or exterior plywood. Simply nail it together and get it square by some means. This can be done with a carpenter's square or anything else with a right angle, such as a book, or merely by adjusting it until the two diagonal measurements are exactly the same. When it's square, nail on temporary braces with small nails, not driving the nails all the way in, so you can pull them out later. These will keep it square while you're fiddling with it. Then try it in your hole or space, depending on your method. It may not fit; if not, adjust the size of the hole or space by hacking with an axe. If you'll be using ready-made sashes, try them in the frame, too, to make sure they'll fit.

When done, put it into position and attach the bottom, checking with a plumb bob to get it vertical. There may be spaces between the frame and the walls if you're fitting the frames into cutout holes. If so, fill these snugly with strips of wood, wood chips, or other nailable material, but not so snug as to force the frame out of square, or the sash won't fit. Then nail it firmly in place.

If you're building around these standing frames, prop each one up with a pole as well as nailing the bottom so that it will stay put while you put subsequent logs in place. Then cut shorter sections of wall logs so that one end abuts flush against the frame, and is held in place by nails or pegs from the inside of the frame. The other end is notched at the corner, as usual. Sections between windows, of course, are attached to frames at both ends. Remember, though, before attaching any of these sections to the frames, to prop each one up 2 inches to leave the usual gap. When you get above the level of the frames, resume building as before.

The same general procedures apply to putting in door frames, except that the doorsill will be right at the height of the floor joists, if any. This may require splitting out part of the sill log as soon as it is laid, if you plan to build the door frame in. If you're planning on a dirt or stone floor, you may want to saw the sill nearly through at that point, to avoid having to step up and then down again any more than necessary. If you do this, though, put extra foundation supports under the sill at each side of the door to make up for the loss of strength.

6
THE ESSENTIAL ROOF

When you've had the experience of living 1½ years without a house, you learn not to take certain conveniences for granted. Without such an experience, it is difficult to realize just what doing without a house means.

By far the worst of the inclement conditions suffered by the houseless is wet, in the forms of damp, rain, snow, sleet, and hail. It is miserable to cook in the rain, or eat in it. Doing dishes is grim, and sleeping may be nearly impossible. Worse yet, though, is the damage to your possessions. You may be only uncomfortable, but clothing, bedding, and books can be damaged or destroyed for good. This can be a disaster if there is no way to replace them.

It is easy to see, therefore, why the roof is just about the most important part of the cabin, and why it pays to invest in a really good one. The roof has always been the most troublesome part to provide from natural materials, and this accounts for the popularity that ready-made commercial roofings have enjoyed since they were first invented. Today, many people aren't aware that a good roof can be had without its materials being bought. But it can indeed, and it's not really a gargantuan feat—only troublesome, as we said before.

Since you have plenty of roof choices, both natural and commercial, consider your limitations—time, materials, money, strength, and needs—and plan carefully, and you'll get a roof that exactly suits them all.

COMPONENTS

The three primary ingredients of a roof are the waterproof covering, the framework that holds it up (and down), and the triangular section of cabin wall at the two ends, which runs up to the peak. The three parts cannot function separately; they must all be suited to one another. For simplicity, we will call the covering the skin; the framework, the bones; and the triangular wall, the endwall. The type of skin you choose will govern the bones you must use, and these will limit your choice of endwall. So remember, when you select your skin you're taking the whole package that goes with it.

NATURAL SKINS

Many a settler, when he had the walls of his cabin up, simply took the canvas cover off his covered wagon and tied it on as a temporary roof. Often, with a family to get under shelter quickly, he would even suit the size of the cabin to that cover from the start. But for a permanent roof he'd make something as sturdy and durable as he possibly could. A frequent choice, where there was sufficient timber, was an overlapped hewn-slab roof. These slabs were boards from 1 to 3 inches thick, produced by hewing flat opposite sides of a log down to the thickness desired. They were made long enough to run the entire length of the house, plus overhang, and each was overlapped halfway, to make sure of shedding rain. Spikes or wooden pegs held them in place. If a good wood was used, the result was a 4-inch thick, insulated, waterproof roof that would last a lifetime.

Naturally, your choice of wood depends on what is available. Hardwoods are much more durable, but also much harder to work. If you use one of the best softwoods—such as white or red cedar, yellow poplar, yellow pine, hemlock, or pitch pine—you may have a product as good or better than many hardwoods. There are white cedar roofs in New England that are two hundred years old and still in pretty good condition, and in the Appalachians, yellow poplar roofs have held up well under wetter conditions. Even average softwoods—such as red maple, red oak, aspen, basswood, and the like—may hold up twenty years.

Some experts contend that untreated wood will last longer than wood that has been painted, creosoted, or varnished, and point to still-intact colonial houses in New England as their proof. While that may well be true of the heartwood of virgin timber, it is probably not true of what is now available. Almost any wood available today will hold up better if treated with a good quality water-base paint or other preservative (or see Chapter 2.)

You will probably be using green wood for your slabs, so they aren't as likely to split when you mount them as seasoned wood. Since green wood shrinks as it dries, across the grain, all the slabs should be overlapped one-half, rather than a smaller amount. What starts out as a one-half overlap in the green wood will end up one-third or less when it has shrunk. A smaller overlap might develop leaks.

When you're putting on the slabs, alternate large ends with small ends. The slabs won't be the same width end to end, because the logs they were hewn from weren't. This way the overlapping edges will follow each other.

Slabs adapt best to vertical purlins (see "Bones," later in this chapter). They should be attached at both ends to the endwall purlins, and to at least one other purlin somewhere in the middle. If you're using nails for the purpose, use large ones, two at each point. The lower nail should connect the current slab to the previous one beneath it, and the upper nail should run directly into the purlin. You can make it even more solid by putting two

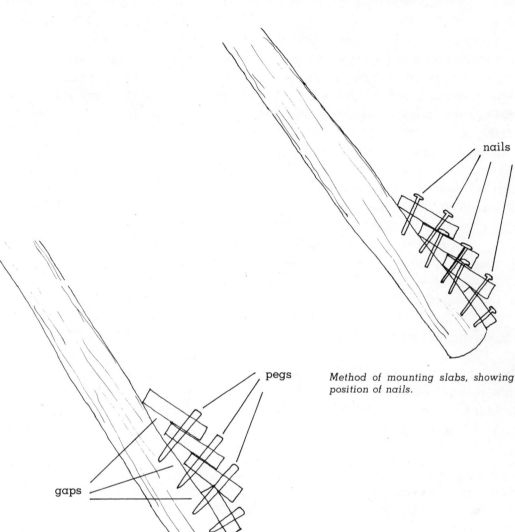

Method of mounting slabs, showing position of nails.

Positioning of pegs in slabs. Note gaps beneath each slab.

nails in the same way into each purlin the slab crosses. Slant the points of all the nails in toward the center of the slab. Then, when the slabs shrink crossgrain, the nails will be able to move with them and retain their firm hold. If you're using pegs, one at each of the three points is sufficient, running through the current slab, the previous slab, and into the purlin.

When you're through, there will be a row of tiny gaps along the endwall purlins, one under each slab. Be sure to chink these carefully, or you'll have a highway for wasps and yellow jackets that would dearly love to nest in your attic.

When you get to the top, make a V-trough by nailing together two slabs, turn it upside down on the roof peak, and attach. If you have no nails, hew out a V-trough from a whole log and invert it and peg.

A second type of wooden roof, the hogshed roof, is made by hewing off one side of a short log, to a depth of perhaps one-third its thickness. The log should be just long enough to reach at a shallow pitch from eaves to ridge-pole of a small cabin. Cut one end off at an angle, so you can nail or peg through the point to hold it to the ridge, and notch the other end over the top of the cabin wall, all with the flat side up. A layer of these is laid flush against one another. Then spread mud, clay, tar, or pine pitch along the flat surfaces, and lay a second layer of logs over the first, flat sides down and cracks offset, to form a ridge-and-valley tile effect. Peg the second layer, cut off at the top in points as before, to the first. The filling between layers prevents rain from running in sideways.

A slight improvement on this method was sometimes made by hewing out V-troughs shallowly down the length of the logs, instead of flat-hewing. Then when the second layer is turned upside down over the first, no chinking is needed because water would have to run uphill to get in sideways.

With either method, this is a very durable roof, although heavy, and has the advantage of being skin and bones all in one. It is practical only on a small cabin, probably no larger than 12-foot square with roof pitch of no more than 30 degrees. Any larger and it will be so time-consuming to lift that it will negate any other advantage. You could make this type of roof lighter by using hewn slabs, but then you've lost the work-saving advantage this roof had to start with.

A log ready for building a hogshed roof.

If you don't have enough sizable timber for a wooden roof, there are other possibilities. The first is a sod roof. Sod is the surface layer of soil and growing grass, so thickly threaded with tiny intertwining roots that it holds together when a piece of it is cut loose. It can be cut in strips or squares, several inches thick, and peeled off the ground. Sod has been used as a roof primarily in prairie areas, where little timber was available and where there were powerful winds and very cold winters. It kept out the wind, kept in the warmth, and even on shallow pitches usually kept out rain, because water does not soak very deeply into ground where there are roots to drink it up. It only had to be made thick enough. Once the sod was cut and put on a roof, the grass was watered and recommenced growing to form a living thatch over the soil, which caused it to shed rain even more.

For cutting sod cleanly, you need a sharp knife or a special turf-cutter, and you must use great care to peel it back without ripping it to shreds.

Then, when cut, roll it up to transport it. Meanwhile, you have gotten ready the bones for this roof, which are solid vertical poles, discussed later in this chapter. The sod is going to be held in place only by gravity and friction, so the roof pitch must be kept very shallow, no more than 15 degrees.

Sod has a tendency to filter bits of dirt down now and then. If you can afford to buy a sheet of black plastic to place over the bones before laying the sod, it will be well worth it. A large piece of cloth would do, as will cardboard, though both will rot in time. But plastic is best, and is rather inexpensive (at this writing a 15×25-foot roll of black plastic was selling for about $11). As an alternative, you could collect slender withes of willow or similar straight brush, and place it several inches thick over and perpendicular to the bones before laying your sod.

If you are using plastic, cloth, or cardboard for this purpose, after putting it in place take additional poles and attach them horizontally over these materials, at intervals matching the length of the pieces of sod you have cut, so that a row of sod will fit between each pole and the next. Friction is greatly reduced by these materials, and the sod will not stay on without help. If you are using brush or nothing at all, you don't need this additional reinforcement.

When you're ready to begin, lay the bottom row solidly, flush together, then the second row, overlapping the first row half, and cracks offset, and so on. When you're completely done, go back and begin again, covering the entire roof a second time. This is time-consuming, but necessary for shedding water, and makes very good insulation as well. Water it as soon as you're done.

A related roof is a dirt roof. It takes the same solid vertical poles at the same shallow pitch. The plastic sheeting or other material is even more helpful here than with sod, but you can also use brush, as before, or straw or grass to minimize sifting.

When your vertical poles are in place, put down your filtering material, then attach horizontal poles as before, about 2 feet apart. If using grass or straw, put this on after the horizontals are attached and pile loose dirt very carefully over all, 8 to 10 inches thick. If possible, seed with a mixture of a good permanent grass, such as Kentucky bluegrass, and a quick-sprouting type, such as rye. Water it, then immediately cover it thickly with brush or straw to keep it from being eroded by wind or water. The rye should come up in two or three days, and will hold the soil until the bluegrass comes up, in several weeks. Then the rye will die off, letting the bluegrass take over, and you'll have a permanent living thatch.

If you can't afford grass seed, and don't have timber or sod, put very stiff mud on the roof instead of loose dirt. (Better yet, if you can, use Magic Cement, Chapter 2.) It should contain just enough moisture so it will not crumble when molded. This should be pressed on over solid vertical poles, as before, but without the extra horizontals. Start at the top of the roof, and make it at least 8 inches thick throughout. Any fibrous material stirred into the mud—such as sawdust, wood chips, straw, pebbles, sand, ground corncobs, dead leaves, pine needles, or the like—will help it cohere and not crack excessively in drying. As you spread the mud, give it a smooth finish with your hand. When this is done, it will be a fair roof, possibly better than fair, depending on the circumstances. It is certain to crack in drying, so when it does, go back up and fill the cracks with more of the same. Or if you can fill them with pitch or related substances, so much the better. Moss and lichens will almost certainly grow on it, and will improve it further by allowing it to breathe.

There is yet another possibility—thatching. Thatching is an ancient method, used extensively in England where they use Norfolk reed, which is considered the finest material in the world for the purpose. A first-class job done with it by an expert can last seventy years.

Over here, however, we must use what we have—straw, long grass, or reeds. It takes vast quantities of whatever is used, and a great deal of durable rope or twine. The job that is likely to be practical for the person in a hurry will probably last only two to fifteen years, depending on what you use and how thickly and carefully you do it. Furthermore, it requires at least a 45-degree roof, and 60 degrees is better.

The general procedure is to use horizontal purlins as bones (see later this

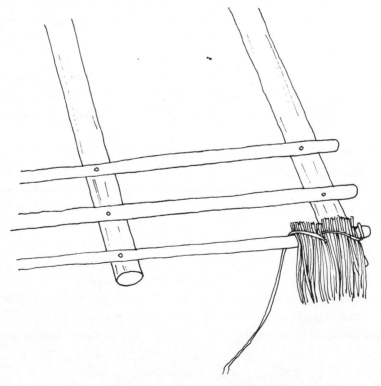

Method of attaching thatch with rope.

chapter) and tie one end of a long rope to one end of the lowest purlin. Then take a 4- to 6-inch-thick bunch of thatching material, which you have wetted and straightened as much as possible, and place its upper end upon the purlin right next to the rope. Now loop the rope first under the purlin, then over the bunch of thatching, then under the purlin again, then up over the next bunch, and so on. Scrunch each bunch tightly up against the previous one as you go. When the bottom row is done, start over and do it again, this time offsetting the cracks. Only the bottom row need be done twice. Each row should overlap the previous row three-quarters. (This is necessary if the roof is to last as long as possible, but it does tend to make difficulties in putting on the bones because they must be spaced so closely—at a distance of about one-fourth the length of your thatching material on the average. Consequently we would not recommend using this roof unless you can obtain nails to attach the bones with, or you somehow happen to have 5,000 feet of nylon rope handy to tie them on. Pegging such a framework would be a life's work.)

In some ways this is the finickiest of roofs. It takes time to do a decent job, and a lot of materials and rope, too, but in a marshy area of nothing but reeds and swamp, it's about the only natural choice.

NATURAL SKINS NOT RECOMMENDED

Many old-time roofs were made from wooden shingles, and shingles are even used today to some extent. They last a long time and are very pleasing, but buying them is a lot different from making them yourself. Even with perfect conditions—straight-grained heartwood from a large tree (2 feet through or more) of the right kind, with few branches or knots, a froe, draw-knife, maul, and shingle-horse—you still need considerable technique and experience.

If by some miracle you have the right timber and tools, and you already know how to rive shingles and enjoy it, and you aren't in any hurry, that's wonderful. But very few people who are building a cabin to live in are likely to meet all these qualifications, and for a person who doesn't meet them to try it can be a heart-breaking experience that can greatly delay the cabin or even prevent its being finished at all. So we are emphatically not recommending it, and are not including any instructions for it. (A variation of shingles, which may be more practical, is discussed later in this chapter.)

A bark roof seems to come to everyone's mind when they think of a quick skin for temporary purposes. We all know how the eastern and northern Indians used them extensively, but what we don't all know is that the Indians had virgin timber that was very thick (wide strips of bark) and very tall, with

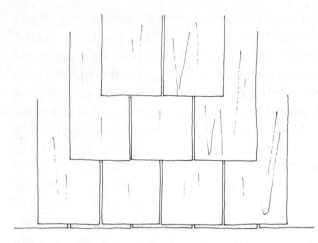

*General method of shingling. Note
the double bottom row.*

smiling

frowning

*Shape of tire shingles for rubber
shingling Method 2.*

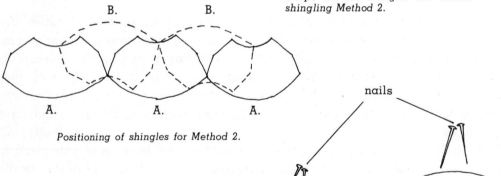

Positioning of shingles for Method 2.

nails

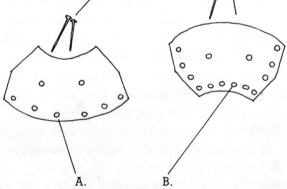

Positions of nails for Method 2.

few low branches (no knots to make the bark tear to pieces while being removed). Furthermore, the Indians had only stone hatchets, so, even though bark removal and use was hard, even with virgin timber it was still easier than hewing 10-foot-thick trees into slabs with stone hatchets. Today, even if you can find suitable trees to take bark from, it is a crime to do it, in most instances, since a tree of such size should be a national treasure. Removing bark usually kills a tree, and even if it doesn't, the bark will never grow back and the tree is disfigured for life.

The only case where it might be both easy and moral to make a bark roof would be if you lived where white birch grows extensively, and you found great numbers of fallen ones with enough bark in good condition on them for a roof. In that case, the bark would probably pull off easily, but if not, remove it with care, as discussed in Chapter 5, prying gently and pounding with a wooden maul around knots when it sticks. Once it is off, lay it on the ground, tan side downwards, and moisture from the ground will flatten it and make it pliable enough to roll up in a short, thick roll and carry it to your site. Before attempting to attach it to your roof, pour hot water on each piece as you need it, to make it pliable enough not to tear too easily. Even then, be at least as careful with it as with tar paper. This is still a temporary roof, and will probably last about a year. If you coat it with pine pitch or the like, it may last several years.

SCAVENGED SKINS AND CHEAP COMBINATIONS

If you have very little money, or none, you may still be able to come by a roof without making one out of natural materials. There are many different types of salvageable materials in dumps all across the country. For example, shingles may be made out of ordinary tin cans by cutting off the bottoms and tops and making a slit down the sides with a small pair of tin-snips. Even better would be using all-aluminum beer and soft-drink cans, since these would never rust.

You could even use thin puncheons or slats, which are the waste product of sawmilled logs. An enormous pile of these can sometimes be obtained very cheaply, maybe even free for hauling them away. Even if you have to go to some trouble to get them, this is still much quicker for the uninitiated than attempting to rive shingles. For bones, you'll need horizontal purlins of one type or the other.

Along the same lines would be a roof of plastic shingles, cut from 8-pound lard buckets, bleach bottles, antifreeze containers, and the like. If you have transportation, you could probably collect enough of these yourself fairly easily. If not, you might be able to persuade neighbor kids or local Boy or

Girl Scouts to collect them for you for a small fee. The only disadvantage of plastic is that the sun does damage it over a period of time, so it wouldn't be quite as permanent as metal.

A shingled roof can also be made from old rubber tires in either of two ways. The first method is easier to understand, but the second gets considerably more mileage out of each tire, and lets you get by with a backing of solid vertical poles.

Method 1: With a hacksaw and knife, cut the sidewalls off each tire, then cut the road surface into four pieces, each of which will be 6 to 8 inches wide and 18 to 24 inches long. Position them one row at a time on your roof, starting at the bottom. Do the bottom row twice, offsetting cracks, and overlap each succeeding row one-third, offsetting all cracks.

Method 2: Saw and cut each whole tire into four pieces, like cutting a pie into fourths, then slice each piece in half flatwise, the way you would slice a bagel. Each of these curved pieces will be a shingle. Position them on the bones by laying all the smiling ones, or *As*, first, as shown in the drawing, with their tips just touching, then lay all the frowning ones, or *Bs*, of that row. Their tips, too, should just touch, and each B should completely cover the gap between two As, and overlap both As. When that row is done, begin laying the As of the second row, each directly in line with an A of the first row, and overlapping it by one-fourth. Each A should have six long-model roofing nails along the longer curving edge, and none anywhere else. Each B should have four nails along each slanted edge, and along its short curving edge, but none on the long curving edge. When you get to the ridge, lay a row over the ridge of pieces all going the same direction, and overlapped one-half.

As you can see, the second method is likely to take quite a few roofing nails, but it also takes fewer tires, and will look very pretty and unusual. All in all, it's the better method of the two.

For any of these shingle ideas, you will need to figure the cost of nails. Where the skin is metal, the nails should be of the same metal as the skin.

The big catch about shingling is the backing needed. Rubber-tire Method 2 lets you get by with solid vertical poles, but if you use plastic or tin can shingles, or rubber-tire Method 1, you will need a solid, flat surface for attachment, and this can be hard to come by. If your only option is homemade natural materials, the one possibilitiy is sawn or hewn slabs. But if you're going to make these, why bother with the shingles? Slabs are sufficient roofing by themselves.

You may be able to salvage a backing. There is old barn wood, which people will sometimes let you have just for tearing the barn down and hauling the wood away. Again, though, if you can get barn wood of decent quality, you don't need the shingles. And, too, tearing down a barn is a lot of work. It may not be worth it.

Another salvage possibility is an abandoned mobile home, or even an abandoned and fallen-down dwelling. Here you may find particle board or fiberboard that come in large sheets. While they are not usable themselves as skins, they will still do fine for shingle-backing. Since they are not put together with marine glues, wet or even damp will dissolve them in time. They will have to be coated with some kind of preservative at least at the edges and undersides of overhangs to prevent moisture absorption.

Mobile homes also offer other useful materials for salvage, the most valuable being the siding and roofing. This is usually aluminum, and certainly waterproof, and if you can get a large enough quantity of it, you need not fiddle with shingles. It can be attached directly to either horizontal purlins or solid vertical poles, depending on the size and shape of the pieces. The only difficulty is in removing it from the mobile home. Rather than trying to unscrew hundreds of screws, go inside and pry off with a crowbar the studding into which they are screwed. Then you can simply carry off the pieces.

Backings can, of course, be purchased if you have the money. You can choose fiberboard or particle board, but either will need weatherproofing. Combining either material with one of the scavenged skins just discussed will result in an excellent roof for a comparatively low cost, though it will certainly take some time to produce shingles or salvage sheet metal.

You should use some type of roofing cement with these various skins. This can be bought in five-gallon cans, or you can use homemade pine pitch. You can also use melted plastic made by setting some plastic article afire, and dabbing it on still hot, although it tends not to adhere to metal.

COMMERCIAL SKINS

One of the most interesting possibilities we have heard of is roofing with cement. Commercially, this is done by pouring or by manufacturing tiles of Portland cement, but neither of these plans is very practical for the log cabin builder. Another method has been used in the Middle East, which is simple enough and works well. Burlap sacks are dipped in a mixture of cement just thick enough to adhere to them, and are then laid over solid vertical poles on a roof of moderate pitch, say 30 to 45 degrees. Each is overlapped sideways one-fourth by its neighbor in the same row and each row is overlapped one-half by the next row, then the entire roof is done over again enough times to produce a uniform 2-inch thickness. The wet sacks sag into the depressions between the poles, and a ridge-and-valley tile effect is produced. The only difficulty is keeping the cement moist enough during drying to prevent cracking. This can be accomplished by placing plastic sheeting over the wet roof and tying it down until the cement slowly dries. If cracks do occur, they can be repaired easily enough with more cement.

There are many other commercial roofings available, if you can afford them. Aluminum sheet roofing, wooden shingles, slate, and tile are among the finest roofs you can buy. If you do plan to buy a roof, be very careful; you might think you're going to get by cheaply, and be mistaken.

Other than cement, the cheapest roof you can buy is exterior grade plywood, which in the long run is even cheaper than tar paper. Both tar paper and asphalt shingles require a solid flat surface beneath. Where will you get that? You may be able to salvage it, but if you're willing to salvage, why not salvage the skin also and save the money? If you buy fiberboard or particle board, the two cheapest options, you'll have to add that cost to that of the tar paper, roofing cement, and nails. When you add that up and compare it to the cost of exterior plywood and nails for the same roof, in most cases you'll find there's hardly any difference. Not only that, but exterior ply is quicker and easier to put up and will last for many years, while tar paper is usually good only for about five years. So, if you want to buy your roof as inexpensively as possible, you should probably choose either cement or exterior ply. And don't consider coating or painting your plywood; it already has a weatherproof finish that is superior to what you could do.

On a 60-degree roof, you can sneak by with ¼-inch plywood; on a 45-degree roof, ⅜ inch; on a 30-degree roof, ½ inch; and on a 15-degree roof, ⅝ inch. You can position the sheets as best they fit to get minimum waste, but start at the bottom and overlap layers about a foot. After an entire side is finished, go back and cap every crack with a strip 1 foot wide. Start at the bottom for this process, too, and as you go up overlap the caps or they'll leak. Do not try capping as you go along; it simply won't work. To cap the ridge, nail 1-foot strips together to form a V-trough. Make as many of these as necessary for the length of the ridge. After spreading tar, pitch, or whatever along both sides of the ridge, turn the troughs upside down and nail down both edges, with each trough overlapping its neighbor sideways. This will be a quick, easy, durable, and beautiful roof.

PITCHES

For a long time now the trend in roofs has been exclusively toward shallow pitches. These have two main advantages: they require the minimum of roofing materials, and they reduce difficulties about raising ridgepoles. But steep pitches have advantages, too. They provide much more usable upstairs living space, and they shed rain and snow much better. Consequently, they last longer and are more maintenance-free. In our opinion they are also much more beautiful.

If you're using modern roofing materials, you may not have to worry about their ability to shed rain, although snow is always a trial for shallow pitches. The upstairs space question still stands, however. While it may be easy to have a housing contractor build a bigger house if you want more space, it is not that easy when you are building your own log cabin. You have to keep it as small as you can get away with because longer logs are heavier logs.

On the other hand, a steeper roof means longer logs for purlins, if vertical, or, if horizontal, more of them. Some natural skins will dictate the pitch you must use, but if you have a choice, at least consider using a steeper pitch than is common, for the reasons already stated. The extra shedding ability, especially with natural skins, is not to be taken lightly. Large families particularly can use the upstairs space, which adapts wonderfully to dormitories or cubicles.

For the person building alone, in a hurry, everything is different. If you have nails, build the smallest possible cabin and make it a lean-to type. This eliminates endwalls, uses minimum roofing, and wipes out all difficulties with raising the ridgepole, since lean-tos don't have ridgepoles. But it does take nails to hold all those slanted joints in place. If you don't have the nails, build an ordinary type, but small and with a shallow roof pitch.

OVERHANGS

To give any cabin a fair chance to last as long as possible, you need a substantial roof overhang. This should be a minimum of 1½ feet (2 feet or more is even better), measured directly sideways out from the wall, not along the slant of the roof. This is going to increase the amount of skin you will need, but it's more than worth it if you plan to occupy the cabin for more than a year or two. Even an emergency cabin should have a 1-foot overhang if at all possible.

There are two ways of making an overhang, depending on the pitch of the roof. If the roof will have a pitch of 35 degrees or less, you can use a natural overhang, which means you can just let the roof continue a certain distance out beyond the wall. If your roof is going to be steeper, letting it extend that way very far would probably make you bump your head on it, or it would interfere with the opening and closing of doors, or block light from windows. And if you don't let it extend that far, you won't get much weather protection for walls or foundation. The best solution is a cantilevered overhang.

Cantilevering begins with the two highest logs of the cabin walls, which we are calling the upper plates. On a rectangular cabin these should be on the short ends, and on a square one on whichever sides you want to be the gable ends. For cantilevering, the upper plates are not made the same length as the rest of the logs of those sides, but longer. The length of your desired overhang, say 2 feet, is added to each end of each upper plate. With a 2-foot overhang, the upper plates would be 4 feet longer than the other wall logs, and centered so that the overhang is equal at both ends. At the same time that you lay the upper plates, you also lay the upstairs floor joists, running parallel to the upper plates and the same length. These should be spaced no farther than 3 feet apart.

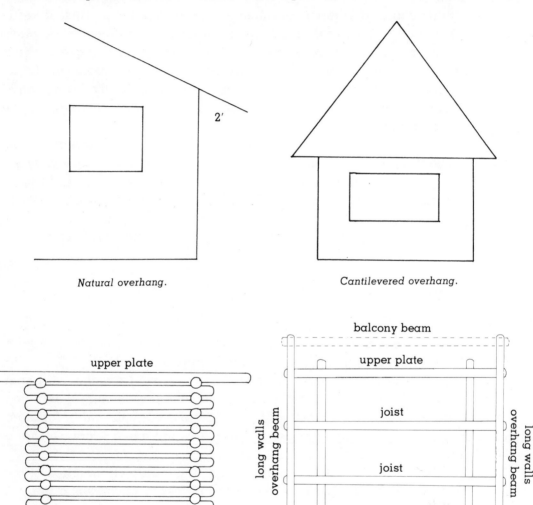

Natural overhang.

Cantilevered overhang.

Extended upper plate for cantilevered overhang.

Layout of basic beams for cantilevered overhang.

Across the very ends of the upper plates and the floor joists, lay the overhang beams, notched over each joist and upper plate. These are the same thickness as the cabin logs, and are long enough to extend 2 feet (or whatever your desired overhang) out beyond each upper plate to provide the overhang for the two ends. Then they are nailed or pegged to each upper plate and floor joist. From there, you build your endwalls and roof as if the overhang beams were really just the tops of your walls.

A cantilevered overhang makes more upstairs space, since it increases the floor size and also raises the peak a little. In addition, it makes a stronger upstairs floor because the weight of the roof rests on the ends of the floor joists, thereby arching them slightly so they'll never sag.

It's possible to extend the overhang even farther to make a front porch and considerably larger upstairs, or even on both sides for front and back porches. In addition, if your upstairs is going to be tall enough, you can make a balcony at one gable end by extending the overhang beams and the ridgepole 3 or 4 feet beyond the end wall instead of 2 feet, and running a balcony beam from one overhang beam to the other. Then just floor in as much of that space as practical and put up a railing. If extra support should be needed, a diagonal brace from the balcony beam down to some point on the wall below will take care of it.

ENDWALLS

There are two practical types of endwalls. Which of them you use will depend on your bones. First is a *solid log endwall*, which can be built with either a natural overhang or a cantilevered one.

For a natural overhang, the upper plates, or the two highest logs, should not be on the short ends as they would be for a cantilevered overhang, but should be on the long sides. They are extended 2 feet beyond the walls, as before. The logs the upper plates are notched over, which are the two highest of the short ends, are called the lower plates. You will be building your endwalls on top of them.

In order not to lift any more logs than necessary, you should measure off and cut on the ground the lengths you will need for your endwalls. Do this by marking out a triangle in the dirt, with stakes and string, poles, or whatever you have, of the same dimensions as your endwall-to-be. Here are the steps: mark out a straight line the length of the cabin's short wall (inside dimension); find and mark the middle point; measure at a right angle from that point up to the height at which you want the peak (inside) and draw diagonals from that peak point to the two ends of the first straight line to complete the triangle.

*Solid log endwall with natural over-
hang. Note that the ends of the lower
plate have been cut very short to allow the purlins to pass over them.*

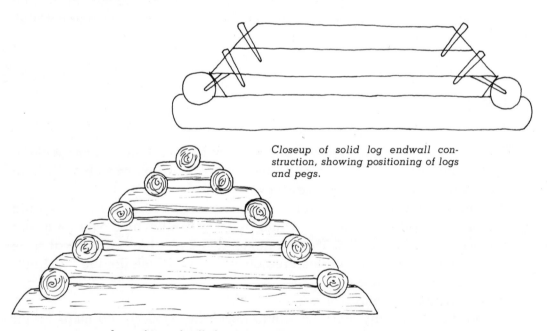

*Closeup of solid log endwall con-
struction, showing positioning of logs
and pegs.*

*Log cabin endwall showing position
of horizontal purlins. Note open-end
notches on endwall logs.*

For solid log endwalls, lay the logs you plan to use on the ground across
the triangle, parallel with the bottom line. Start at that bottom line and fill
the triangle solidly. Then cut off all the log ends right along the diagonal
lines you've marked, and they'll be ready. Cut another log, a 4-inch one this
time, and make it the same length and cut off at the same angle as the longest one of the triangle. If you're going to be using pegs to attach these, in-

stead of spikes, stop and whittle enough of them to have one at each end of each log, and long enough to reach deeply into the one beneath to hold firmly.

When you're finished, take the 4-inch log up and place it upside down directly on top of the lower plate. Peg or spike through each end to the upper plates. Then set the longest 6-inch log on top of it, right side up, and peg.

You may have to wedge one with chips or the like to make it hold still. Or, if you have nails, you can tack it lightly with small ones temporarily. The pegging or spiking must be very firm.

The second log is attached to the first in exactly the same way, and so on. If your shortest log doesn't have room on its top to hold the ridgepole or board, notch it in until you have a space wide enough to receive the ridgepole or board, and then attach the log to the endwall.

To make a cantilevered overhang with solid log endwalls, the procedure is the same except that instead of making the bottom line of your triangle the length of the short wall, you make it the complete length of the upper plate between overhang beams, which, for the purposes of cantilevering, is on the short side.

The second type of endwall is the *log cabin type*. This is built just as the log cabin walls are, with the tips chopped off at an angle in advance and the corners notched. Horizontal purlins are automatically supplied, but their spacing varies with the roof pitch and cannot be controlled. Consequently, you may or may not be able to use them with your intended skin, depending on the spacing that skin requires. On a 30-degree roof, the distance from centers will be 13 to 14 inches, on a 45-degree one, approximately 12 inches, and on a 60-degree roof, approximately 9 inches.

To calculate distances on centers of the purlins for other roof pitches, you need compass, ruler, pencil, and paper. On paper, construct to scale a triangle with the dimensions and angles of your proposed endwall, using the same methods given earlier for doing it on the ground. Use a scale no smaller than ½ inch = 1 foot for accuracy. Draw a vertical line from the peak to the exact center of the base, and make marks all along it (the vertical line) at 6 inches, then 3 inches, then 6, then 3, and so on, starting at the bottom. Draw parallel horizontal lines passing through each of those points to represent your endwall logs and gaps. At both ends of each gap carefully draw a circle 6 inches (to scale) across to show the ends of the horizontal purlins, then measure the distance diagonally between the centers of two of these. Converting this measurement from scale will give you the approximate distance between centers of the actual purlins at your desired pitch. This will give you something to go on, so you can adjust the pitch, perhaps, or use a different type of bones.

If you find that you can use this kind, you have to lay out a triangle on the ground just as before to precut your logs. When you lay the endwall logs across this triangle, be sure to leave gaps of 3 inches between each and the next, for those gaps will be there when they're put in place. Without them you won't be able to get the right lengths.

When you notch the undersides of these, use a different notch from before. Start 6 inches in from the tip of the point, and either saw or chop a cut about 2 inches deep. Then just knock out the wood from there to the end to make an open-ended notch. For the purlins themselves, use the same inverted saddle notch as for the walls, without the open end.

RAISING THE RIDGE

The ridgepole or ridgeboard is the highest point on a roof, except on a lean-to cabin. Its purpose is to provide an anchor point for vertical purlins for ease in erecting them, and as an additional support for various skins. Raising it can be quite a stumbling block unless you consider the problem well in advance.

This problem can be avoided entirely by building a lean-to cabin that doesn't have a ridgepole. For a person alone, this is a very good idea, provided you have the nails. If you don't have the nails, or if you don't want to build a lean-to for some other reason, you can still save trouble by making the roof pitch no steeper than necessary and making sure that the ridgepole is no higher above the tops of the walls than your own height. That way, you can easily stand up and lift it into place. In working with it, it will help to roughly floor in your upstairs with logs notched over the joists, at least at the two ends, to give you a place to stand and work. You can also minimize weight by using a slab turned on edge for a ridgeboard, instead of using a log.

If you're building a large and tall cabin, you won't have ridgepole problems on a cabin with horizontal purlins. Since you start from the bottom it is easy to raise each successive purlin using all the previous ones as steps. That goes for the ridgepole, too, but with vertical purlins or solid vertical poles, you need help.

Start by roughly flooring in the ends of the upstairs. Make sure the logs you use for this are the same thickness as your cabin logs; since they won't be nailed, only their mass will keep them from skidding. Next, construct a scaffolding by running two poles diagonally from a point about a foot below the peak to two points 4 feet apart and each 2 to 4 feet out from the wall. Nail these securely in place. Then proceed to attach horizontal poles around the three sides of that area, at 1-foot intervals, for rungs. All of the poles used must be strong enough to hold your weight at that span. When you're done, you'll have a three-sided, pointed ladder at each end of the cabin. Then all you have to do is get your ridgepole or board up onto the floor joists by whatever means you've been using to get your cabin logs up onto the wall. Now raise it one end at a time, not alternating ends, until you can place it on top and affix it.

This scaffolding can be constructed with pegs, of course, but it is much more laborious. Tying it together after notching the diagonals to receive each horizontal is easier than pegging, but nails are really the way. If you don't have the nails, make a point of not building the roof too steep for you to stand up and lift the ridgepole.

The three-sided ladder for raising the ridgepole, and the beaming for a cantilevered overhang in place.

THE BONES

Bones that run slanting from the height of the walls up to a higher wall or to a ridgepole or board are called vertical; those that run sideways from one endwall to the other are called horizontal. Remember that they all should be barked, just as the cabin logs were.

Verticals   *Vertical purlins.* With solid leg endwalls. For sawn or hewn slabs, plywood, or particle board backing with various types of shingles.

These are parallel poles of about the same thickness as the cabin logs, spaced from 3 to 5 feet apart, depending on the size of the cabin and the material to be used with them, and of whatever length is needed to provide sufficient overhang at the desired pitch. If they are being run to a ridgepole or board, each purlin is cut off at a slant at the upper end, and a nail or peg driven through the point to attach it to the ridge. The lower end is notched over the upper plate for a natural overhang, or over the overhang beam for a cantilevered one. In either case it is also nailed or pegged in place there. Purlins are placed exactly opposite each other for proper support of the roof.

Solid vertical poles. For rubber shingles (Method 2), sod, dirt, or cement.

These are essentially the same as vertical purlins, except that there are many more of them, and they are not spaced, but crowded as closely together as possible to form almost solid cover. Where the span is to be short, and the cabin small (say, 12-foot square or less), they may also be of smaller diameter than the cabin logs. On larger cabins. they should be just about the same.

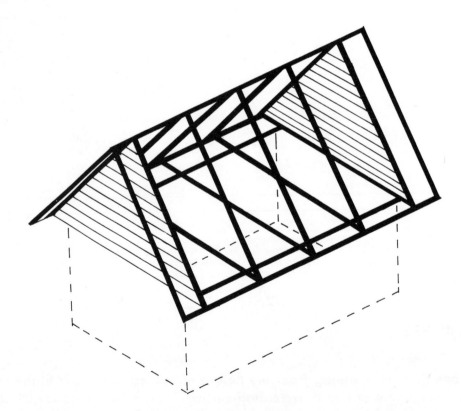

Vertical purlins.

Horizontals *Plain horizontal purlins.* With solid log endwalls. For plywood, particle board, or fiberboard backing with various types of shingles, sheet metal, or thatching. Here too, the thickness should be the same as the cabin logs, since they will be running the same distance, often unsupported. To make them, build your solid log endwalls as described earlier. Mount the ridgepole and attach it. Then place *vertical purlins* along both slanted edges of each endwall, extending down far enough to provide overhang, and attach with pegs or nails.

If your cabin will be over 12-foot square, position additional vertical purlins at this time from 5- to 8-foot intervals along the wall. Make shallow notches all along the tops of each of these vertical purlins, at the measured intervals which your skin requires. Be very careful about measuring these, and make each purlin exactly like the next. When in doubt, make your notches a little closer than you think you'll need, since at worst that will just allow for a little extra overlap. Take your designated horizontals and lay one at a time across, and nail or peg in place. Remember that these horizontals must be cut long enough to give proper overhang at each end. Start laying these from the bottom, and as each is permanently attached, you can

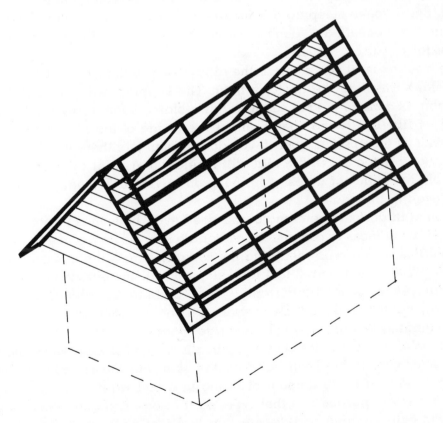

Plain horizontal purlins.

use it as a ladder step for you to climb and to help you raise each succeeding one.

Log cabin horizontals. For all the roofs listed above, except thatched.

This was mostly described earlier under log cabin endwalls, since they are produced simultaneously. If the spacing at your desired pitch makes it possible for you to use this roof, it will result in a rather simple and enormously strong, cohesive roof.

THE LAST LICKS

The instructions so far should be sufficient for entirely putting on the roof. After your cabin is finished, however, you may want to insulate the roof. Modern builders often provide insulation for the roof while they're building it, but you may find it more expedient to get under a roof as quickly as possible and insulate later.

Insulation of the roof can be an advantage or a disadvantage. If you plan on sleeping upstairs, you will need it, if only in the summer, unless your cabin is really in deep shade all the time, which has many other disadvantages. But if you're sleeping downstairs and hoping to store produce in the attic as the pioneers did, don't insulate the roof or it will be too hot in the winter for produce.

The solution is, if you sleep in the attic, insulate the roof; but if you sleep downstairs, insulate the upstairs floor. The simplest way to insulate after the cabin is done is to take sawn or hewn slabs, boards, plywood, particle board, or fiberboard and sheath either the inside of the attic ceiling or the underside of the upstairs floor. If you do a careful job, there will be a certain amount of trapped air within that will insulate to a point by itself. This will probably be sufficient unless you insist on having a 75-degree bedroom at night even in the winter.

If you're in an extreme climate and need even better insulation, you can insert straw or moss or commercial materials into the space. If you have vertical purlins, place your sheathing horizontally across them, starting at the bottom. When you get up 2 to 4 feet, stop and fill the cavity with whatever material you're using. Stuff firmly, then continue sheathing. Stop again every several feet and stuff. Don't wait until you're almost all the way up before beginning to stuff, or you'll never get done.

With solid vertical poles, you can sheath without filling, since the poles themselves constitute filling between the skin and the sheathing. But you can try to force a small amount of filling in if you want.

For horizontal purlins of either type, start at one end and sheath a space with vertically running boards, etc., up to 4 feet wide, from floor to peak.

Then stuff sideways. Sheath another 4-foot width, and then stuff again, and so on.

Another solution to the insulation problem might be dormers. These are easy to add afterwards, at your leisure. All you have to do is construct a frame to support the roof, sides, and actual window on top of your roof at the spot you have selected and marked out.

It is advisable to pick a fair-weather period for this project, since you're going to have to cut a hole in your roof at some point. You can wait, if you wish, until the whole structure is completed, provided you have a chainsaw. But with an ordinary Swedish saw, where you will have to chop a hole with an axe to get it started, it is wiser to do it at the start.

When the frame is finished, attach the siding, which can be the same as the roof's skin or can be overlapped slabs, etc., and fit the window. The windowsill should slant down outwards, to drain water. The only thing to be careful of is flashing, which is the process of sealing joints against leakage. Wherever the dormer joins the roof is a potential leak, and you have to take care that all materials are properly overlapped, daubed with roofing cement, pine pitch, plastic, or the like, to ensure the seal. Last, be sure the dormer's roof has its own little overhang of about 6 inches to protect it.

7

OPENINGS AND CLOSINGS

WINDOWS

Many people in history did not have windows. For one thing, glass was not widely produced until the Renaissance, and a hole in the wall without glass certainly made things a lot colder in winter. Heat loss was considered much more important than light. Even several hundred years later, during Colonial times in this country, glass windows were kept to a minimum because of luxury taxes on them; and when window taxes were no more, glass was still comparatively expensive, and considered a luxury. Thus, even the houses of the rich often had only a few small windows. Screens did not come into common use until the beginning of the twentieth century.

So windows are not the simple necessity we have been accustomed to think them. If you can't afford glass or plastic, you can cut a simple hole to be left open in good weather, and close it with a shutter when faced with inclement conditions.

You can wait until the cabin is up before cutting out your hole, holding the logs in place while you're cutting by the pole-and-tie method, but taking care to include in your tying one log above and one log below those being cut out. When the hole is cut, frame only the two vertical sides with either puncheons or slabs, pegged or nailed. Now all it needs is a method of opening and closing it.

One way of doing this is to drive two vertical posts into the ground or attach them to the floor and ceiling. In either case they should be about 6 inches from the wall, and even with the edges of the hole. Then just fill the area between the posts and the wall with horizontal logs, one on top of another, to above the top of the window hole. You can open it part way by removing some of the top logs. In cold weather, chink some or all of the cracks. To achieve a better fit, you can flatten the top and bottom surfaces of the logs if you wish.

Another way is to make a wooden shutter in the same way as a batten door, described in the "Doors" section of this chapter, only make it smaller. You can use hewn slabs or puncheons installed in any of three ways.

The first way is merely to lift it in and out, with no hinge of any kind.

Shuttle latches can be used to hold it in place. A couple of pegs, strips, or poles attached to the sides or top and bottom of the frame will serve as stops to keep it from falling outwards.

The second way is to use a dowel hinge attachment. With this method the shutter is made as described above, except that one of the battens, whose thickness must be at least ¾ inch, is left long enough to protrude 3 inches beyond both edges of the shutter. Then both protruding ends are whittled down to a diameter of ¾ to 1-inch round, to form peg ends. (If you have a choice of wood for this batten, choose hard or soft wood of a twisty grain.) Each peg end is then fitted into a notch just slightly bigger than itself, which you carve into the inside cabin wall from the side, rather than drilling from above, for ease of insertion. Finally, wooden strips, poles, or slabs are attached across the open fronts of the notches to hold the pegs in.

You can place the peg-batten horizontally at the top of the shutter, so it opens upwards, or at one edge running vertically to open sideways, or in the center, either vertically or horizontally, so it pivots. This last choice will not do if you have any plans for installing screen later on, since then it wouldn't open all the way.

You can also use strips of leather or tire rubber for conventional-type hinges. Just cut pieces 4 or 5 inches square, and place them at two or three

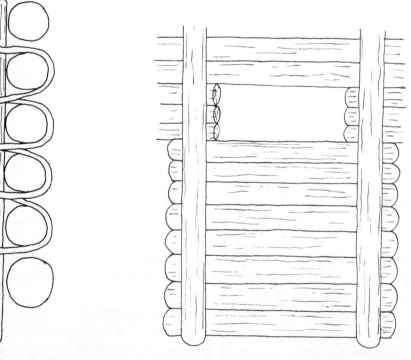

The pole-and-tie method of holding logs still while cutting out holes.

Primitive window closing with logs stacked in front of opening.

points along one edge. Attach them to shutter and wall with washers and screws or big nails.

One step beyond the simple shuttered window is the same window with screen tacked on. Though it is still necessary to close it in cold weather, and so sacrifice light, at least you have protection from insects, particularly mosquitoes, in warm weather.

If you can also afford clear flexible plastic, you need not make the shutter unless you want to. A window of screen and plastic, though it may look primitive, catapults you into modern times convenience-wise. You can attach the plastic permanently for six months of the year, with wooden strips and either small nails or pegs, like the screen, or you can build a frame to mount it. You may even be able to devise some ingenious method of raising and lowering the plastic without a frame. It is certainly an advantage to be able to open or close it at will, though that, too, is something only recently made common.

This screen-and-plastic combination is also an excellent temporary solution while you're taking the time to build more complicated sash. If really cold weather catches you out, you can always attach a second layer of plastic as a storm window, nailed with the screen on the natural ledge of the window frame.

MORE SOPHISTICATED WINDOWS

In this context, more sophisticated really means both more complicated and more convenient in the long run. Flexible plastic will last for some years if carefully treated, but ordinary glass, plate glass, and Plexiglas are more durable and require less care.

Plate glass is quite expensive, though it can sometimes be salvaged, as in car door windows, store front windows, and sliding glass doors. It is extremely tough, however, hard to break, and fairly insulative. It also comes in large, easy-to-work-with sheets. If you can get it, it is the best material of all for permanent windows.

Plexiglas, which is thick, hard, perfectly clear plastic, is also expensive. Plexiglas isn't easily broken, but is easily scratched. It's easy to work with, can be drilled and screwed into position, and doesn't conduct cold like glass, making storm windows unnecessary. However, it lets through harmful ultraviolet rays in a way that glass does not, though a shady location, roof overhang, and curtains would lessen such effects.

Ordinary glass is much cheaper than either plate glass or Plexiglas, even if you buy enough for storm windows, too. But it breaks very easily, and takes great care in cutting and handling. Still, it is the universal window material, and a good one.

To hold any of these materials, you must build sash, or frames, to be movable and removable. If sash are made larger than a certain size, they are too rickety and spread out to hold up. So, depending on the various sizes of your window openings, you will probably have to divide many of your windows into two or more sash. Two-foot sections are really ideal, so in a 4-foot window you would have two sections. The height of a single sash can be up to 5 feet, so probably you won't need to divide vertically.

Extra vertical supports are needed in windows wider than 4 feet. One of these can be a two-by-four or slab wedged firmly in the middle, turned to obscure the least possible light, or it can be a log section if you don't mind the sacrifice of light. Such supports must be put in place and attached first, before any building of sash is begun, because the space they occupy will change the size of your sash. In planning your sash sizes, always take measurements after putting in a middle support. When a support falls in the middle of what would otherwise have been a window sash, recalculate the divisions. For example, a 6-foot-wide window would be expected to divide into three 2-foot sections, but since a middle support is necessary, you would instead make it into four 1½-foot sections. If the width is over 8 feet, put in two equally spaced supports.

OPENING

Sash can be hinged to open sideways, for casement windows, or upwards to be hooked at the ceiling. The latter way saves more space, since it opens out of the way altogether. The former are not likely to lie entirely flat against the wall when opened wide, unless you made sure when framing the hole that your frame was flush with the inside wall logs.

On a window where there are more than two sash, it's not practical to make them all casement-type, since the middle ones when opened would either close off the outside ones or would stick straight into the room at the middle support. You can have the middle ones open upward, while the outside ones open either way, or you can hinge the middle sash to the outside ones, so they open accordion-wise, like folding doors. Or you can also just not open the middle sash.

At every seam where sash come together when closed, wooden or rubber tire strips should be attached all along the back of one of each pair coming together, wide enough to provide a weather seal. The exception here is in the case of accordion-opening windows. With these, attach thin fixed posts in the window frame itself. Strips must also be attached to the window frame at top, bottom, and sides to serve as stops and seal out drafts.

HINGES

You can use the same basic types of hinges for your sash as for the earlier shutter, rubber or leather squares (doubled, in the case of leather), commercial hinges if suitable in strength, or dowel hinges.

To use the dowel method, do not rely on a batten here. Instead, drill holes into the sash, at least ⅜ inch, and fit slightly loose pegs into them. Then carve notches into the frame and perhaps the wall also to receive the pegs, as before, and block off the notches afterwards from the front, so the pegs can't fall out. It's a good idea to use a little linseed oil here every so often.

LATCHES

The simplest ways to latch a window are with hooks or shuttle latches. Shuttle latches are merely small flat pieces of wood with a nail or loose peg through them, attached just loosely enough that the pieces of wood, or shuttles, can swivel to hold the window closed or let it open.

For handles to pull open the windows, you can attach metal rings, headed pegs, or whatever you can devise.

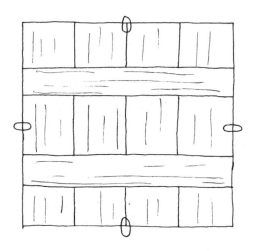

Wooden shutter held in place by shuttle latches.

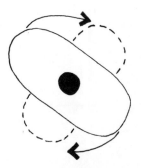

The principle of a shuttle latch.

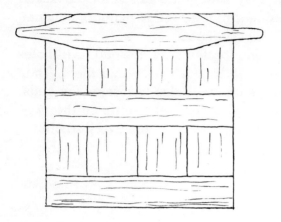

Dowel-hinged shutter.

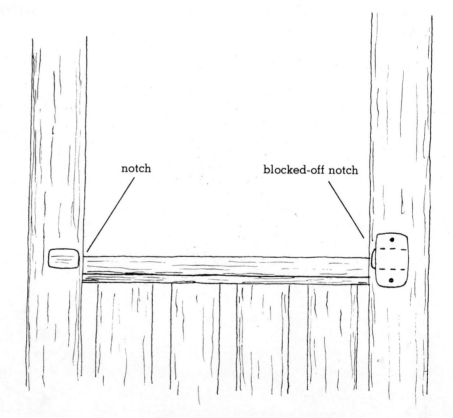

notch

blocked-off notch

The positions of notches for dowel-hinge method; also notch blocked off.

BASIC AND COMPOSITE SASH

An ideal window lets in light at all times, air when desired but only then, and bars insect entrance. The glass or plastic provides the light, an efficient method of closing and opening controls the air circulation, and screen keeps out insects. Wooden bars on the outside give security against marauders of whatever species (except angry bears).

The screen and bars need to be separated some distance from the glass or plastic, and neither need be easily removable. So that leaves the window and storm window, if desired, to be incorporated in a serviceable sash.

You can buy these, of course, as everyone does for conventional houses. It saves time, but is extremely expensive proportionately, costing several times as much as if you made them yourself. The time factor need be no problem, either, if you put up a temporary window in the meantime. We would definitely recommend that you make your own.

The following types of permanent sash are adaptable to one layer of glass or two, so if you want storm windows, they are automatically incorporated. This means they are not removed in warm weather. This saves twice-yearly shuffling, and ensures that any time you shut your window you shut out all drafts, whatever the time of year.

We've given methods for commercial materials only. This is because it takes a great deal of labor to produce suitably finished wood for the purpose out of natural materials. It can certainly be done, though, if you take the time to carefully choose, cut, season, and shape your wood. Once done, follow the directions for plain board sash.

PLAIN BOARD SASH

The pieces of the sash should be about ¾ inch thich and 1½ to 2 inches wide. You can also use two-by-four wood, cut to the same dimensions. First lap-joint the frame together, and nail with nails long enough to clinch on the other side. (See description of clinching under "Doors.") Then mark off a ledge ¼ inch wide and deep enough to accommodate glass, putty, and points, if you plan to use them. (Points are triangular metal pieces made to hold the glass in place and stabilize during puttying and drying.) One-fourth inch deep should be sufficient for this, or less if not using points. With chisel and mallet remove the wood along your lines to produce the ledge. Now lay the glass in place, and either push points or small nails in with your thumb or putty knife, or nail on wooden or rubber tire strips, so that they overlap the glass and hold it in securely. Be very delicate if nailing, or the glass may break from the shock of the hammer. This is a very good method, maybe better than points. Finally, if using points, apply putty to cover them. A substitute for commercial putty may be made using magic cement mixed with pine pitch.

To fit a storm window in the same sash, cut rabbet joints on both back and front as described, and fit glass in both.

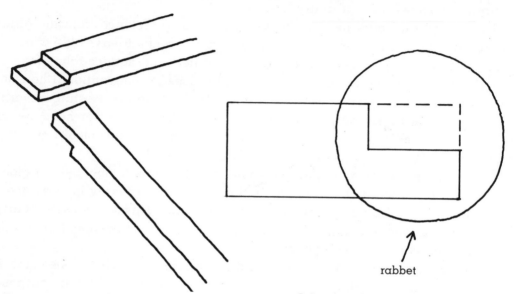

rabbet

How a lap joint is made.

A lap-jointed sash with rabbet joint carved out.

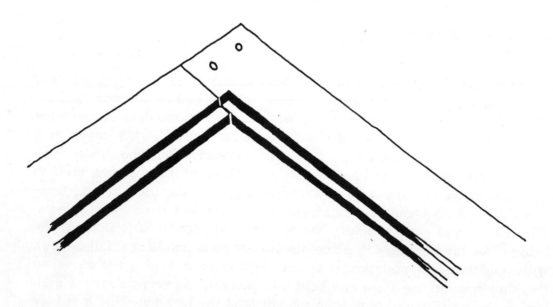

Closeup of rabbet-joint principle.

TONGUE-AND-GROOVED-BOARD SASH

This, too, is lap-jointed, but here you take advantage of the already exist-ing groove to hold the glass in place. Put the two sides and the bottom to-gether, having first removed the tongues from all four pieces with a saw, drawknife, or other means. Then slide the glass down into the three-sided frame from the top, and push putty, clay, or any homemade gunk into the groove to stabilize the glass. Then nail the top on carefully, and putty it.

To make this with a storm window, just make the frame double thickness, two layers of tongue-and-grooved boards, and slide two panes of glass down as described above.

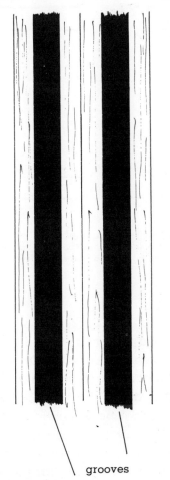

grooves

Method of making dual-glass sash
with tongue-and-grooved boards.

PLYWOOD SASH

With plywood, due to its layered construction, you can't cut a rabbet joint as with board, but you can construct a ledge by placing one frame on top of another, one extending farther toward the middle than the other. The top frame is of ¼-inch plywood, and the bottom one of ½-inch. The two are held together without lap-jointing by laying out the pieces of the lower frame as shown, and laying those of the upper frame on top of them, as shown. Then it is nailed and clinched, not only at the four corners, but in the middle of each side as well. To put in the glass, use the method given under "Plain Board Sash" that best suits. (Remember to use a finishing saw to cut the ¼-inch plywood or it will tear up.)

To incorporate a storm window, attach another identical ¼-inch layer to the back of the ½-inch layer, and put glass in it as described.

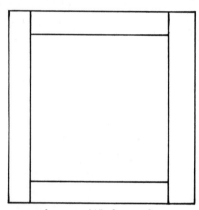 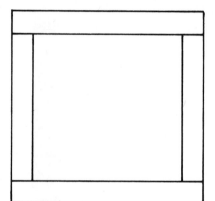

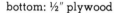

bottom: ½" plywood   top: ¼" plywood

The two parts of a plywood sash, showing how all the separate pieces must be positioned before nailing.

DOUBLE-SASH WINDOWS

If you want to go the whole way, you can also fit your screen and window bars into their own frame. This can then be easily removed for cleaning, but its main advantage is that you can attach screen and bars on the ground instead of at some uncomfortable angle. This frame can be hooked into position from the inside, and so cannot be removed from the outside.

In making this, it isn't necessary to divide up the opening into smaller frames, as for the earlier sash, since the window bars strengthen it sufficiently. But you are still limited by the size that you can lift in and out easily, which for most people will probably be about 4×4 feet. Vertical supports are not necessary, either, but you will probably have to attach light nonsupportive vertical strips every so often, for attaching the screen, which usually comes no wider than 36 inches.

If you aren't planning on having window bars, don't bother making a second sash for the screen alone because it would be uselessly troublesome. You'd have to make several small sash again, since there wouldn't be any bars to strengthen a large frame. Anyway, screen doesn't really need to be removable.

After you make this sash, according to any of the methods given earlier, attach the screen to its inside edge with wooden strips for permanency, and nail the bars onto the outside edge in the pattern and size you have chosen. Just remember to first attach all those bars running in one direction, then all those running the other, and nail at every point where two cross.

The bars can be made of various materials. You can use small green poles, ¾ to 1 inch thick, or you can buy ½- to ¾-inch dowel rods, provided you can find them long enough. Even ½ inch is very strong once they are all interconnected. A third way is to have a lumber mill cut ¾-inch square strips from two-by-fours. Don't try to do this by hand—it would take you forever unless you have access to an electric bench saw. One caution with this, though: you'll have to treat such strips with some preservative, such as paint, stain, or linseed oil. Aluminum strips or pipe can also be used, although they are much more difficult to attach. Whichever way you choose, the looks will be very nice.

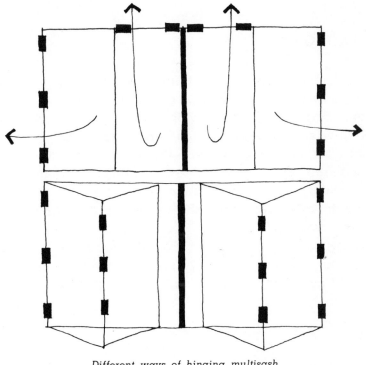

Different ways of hinging multisash windows.

There are limitless patterns to choose from—Elizabethan diamond pattern, square American Colonial, rectangular Georgian Colonial, and so forth. Gothic is the result of combining straight and diagonal lines in various ways. Whichever pattern you choose, experiment with drawings to scale on paper to determine the right size to make them. With Elizabethan, for example, the diamonds are usually best spaced 9 inches apart horizontally, and 2 feet high.

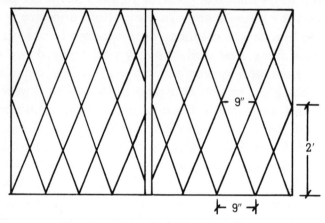

The best dimensions for the diamonds of an Elizabethan pattern of bars.

SALVAGED WINDOWS

If you have a knack for this sort of thing, you can come up with many interesting arrangements using salvaged glass or plastic. For example, there are clear plastic bottles and jars in which varnish and peanut butter come, among other things. These can be cut up to provide a reasonably see-through window. Car windows are excellent-quality plate glass, and some people have managed to mount a whole door into a wall, mechanism intact, and just rolled the window open and closed. This would be a rather sorry-looking solution for a beautiful log cabin, however. You can also remove the glass from a car door, and mount it in a frame in combination with other such pieces to form a rather exotic window reminiscent of stained-glass creations. Sometimes, too, you can salvage sash, complete with glass, from condemned buildings. Shower doors and sliding glass doors are excellent as well.

DOORS

For cutting and framing the hole, follow the directions given in Chapter 5. Remember to arrange the height of the doorsill so that you need not step up or down anymore than necessary in entering. Keep in mind the height of your future floor for this, and cut into the sill log if necessary. And remember that a good door size can be anywhere from 2 to 2½ feet wide and 6½ to 7 feet high.

BATTEN DOORS

The simplest and most appropriate door for a log cabin is some kind of batten door. This is made with boards or puncheons held together with cross-pieces, called battens, and either clinched nails or pegs. (A clinched nail is a nail long enough that it sticks out the other side after being nailed through. It is then beaten over flat and tight with a hammer.) Most of us associate batten doors with barns and sheds, but at one time nearly all doors were made that way. They are quite beautiful in a rustic sort of way, and are very strong.

TWO- OR THREE-BATTEN DOOR

The materials for this can be puncheons, slabs, plain boards, or two-by-fours laid flat. Take as many of these as necessary, laid together and running vertically, to fill the measurements of your framed opening, minus about ⅛ inch on all sides. Across them, nail or peg either two or three battens, as you choose. Clinch all nails.

With anything except puncheons, nail thin strips of wood or rubber tire over all the cracks on the outside to keep out drafts.

With puncheons, turn the round sides outward, and attach the battens to the flat side. When finished, chink the cracks on the outside with some sort of gunk, whether melted plastic, pine pitch, fiberglass, or whatever, to keep out weather. Apply this to the door while it's laying down, and let it dry there before standing it up. And use as little of this as will do the job, for

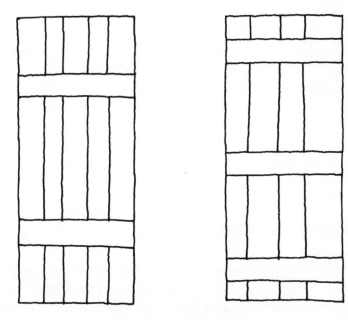

Two- and three-batten doors.

the best appearance of the door. This makes a particularly lovely door, very much in keeping with a log cabin.

Z-BATTEN DOOR

Any version of the above doors can be made both stronger and more beautiful by the addition of diagonal braces, one long one for a two-batten door, or two short ones for a three-batten door.

 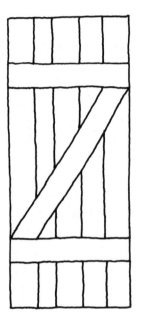

Z-batten doors.

SHEATHED DOOR

This is a double-thickness door, so you can use thinner boards if you want, such as commercial tongue-and-grooved boards. Lay out your vertical boards or puncheons as before, but instead of attaching only two or three battens, completely cover the flat surface with battens, all running horizontally. This removes the necessity for weather-stripping, and is quite strong and nice looking.

ABOUT COMMERCIAL MATERIALS

Particle board should not be used for a door because of its tendency to dissolve in damp or wet. Exterior plywood can be used, if it is ¾ inch thick, but unless you have a piece that size left over, it is cheaper to make a door out of two-by-fours. Enough of these for a door would run you about $15, while a sheet of ¾-inch exterior plywood would cost about $20, and the two-by-fours would be twice as thick and much prettier.

You can also seal out drafts by attaching a piece of sheet metal over the entire surface of the door. If you do this, put it on the inside, so it doesn't spoil the rustic look of the cabin. On the inside, you may be able to decorate it with designs.

HINGES

To hang your door, you can use the dowel-hinge principle, mentioned earlier, or make hinges out of rubber tires or leather, or buy hinges. If you buy, the best are large, heavy T-hinges or barn hinges. T-hinges will be easier to use if you have the choice. For hinges of rubber or leather, use pieces 4×8 inches with rubber, and with leather, either two 4×8-inch pieces used together, or a 4×16-inch piece doubled. It goes without saying that such leather had better be plenty thick and tough.

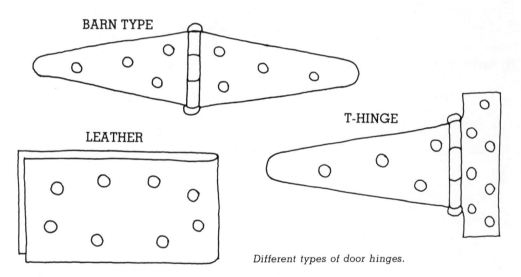

Different types of door hinges.

HANGING A DOOR

Attach the hinges to the door battens on the ground. With bought hinges, use screws; with leather or rubber, use bolts with washers at the door and screws with washers at the door frame, or headed pegs, blind-wedged tightly into both door and frame. Use two pegs at the door and two at the frame on each hinge.

Lift the door into place to see how it fits the hole. If it doesn't, take it back down and make adjustments with wood rasp, saw, or hatchet, and try again. When it fits properly, equalize the door in its frame from top to bottom and side to side by wedging it with chips. Then prop it with a pole while you work on it.

With bought T-hinges, mark on the frame the positions of the screw holes with nail or pencil, then swing the hinge out of the way and drill holes for the screws or punch them with a nail. They can be much smaller than the diameter of the screws themselves. Swing the hinge back and screw in the screws, starting with the middle hinge, middle screw, on a three-batten door, or the top hinge, middle screw, on a two-batten door. On a three-batten door, do the top hinge next, and the bottom one last. With leather or rubber hinges, punch your holes with nails, right through the hinge into the wood, then put in the screws with washers.

If you're using barn hinges, one arm will be attached to the batten, but the other arm is too long to be attached solely to the door frame, as with other hinges. It will have to be attached to the wall as well. As you will be able to see when you have the door standing in place, with its hinges attached to it, you can't get the two arms to line up flat as they should because the battens stick farther into the room than the wall or the door frame. To solve this problem at all the hinge points at once, the easiest way is to peg or nail a slab to the wall and over the frame. The slab should be just thick enough to bring that other hinge arm up level with the one on the door. Make the slab of green hardwood or green twisty softwood if possible, definitely not two-by-four or seasoned board, and the same height as the door frame. Line it up exactly along the crack between the door frame and the door, peg it

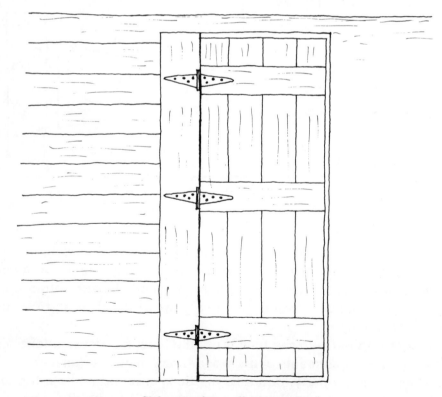

Slab pegged to wall is necessary for attaching a door with barn hinges.

very securely, and proceed. When the door is hung, attach wooden strips at top and sides to seal out drafts, but at the doorsill, attach a slab to the sill itself, occupying the whole surface of the sill up to the edge of the closed door. This will serve the same purpose of preventing drafts, but is not as likely to cause stumbling as a narrow strip nailed there.

MAKING AND HANGING A DOWEL-HINGED DOOR

The procedure for for making this is the same as for an ordinary door, except that the end slab or puncheon (we don't recommend commercial materials here) is left longer than the others by about 4 inches at both bottom and top. Put this longer one at the side where you want the hinges, naturally. If possible, make this piece of good hardwood or at least a twisty softwood, such as red maple or sycamore. In either case, it should be green. Whittle each protruding end abruptly down to a peg, but take care that your pegs are not in line with the very edge of the door, but an inch or so in from it. If they were at the very edge, the door would not open. When that's done, take your knife and round off the inside corner of that edge slightly, includ-

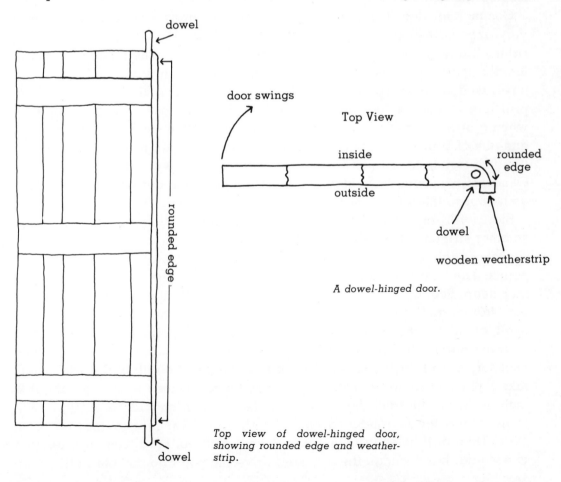

A dowel-hinged door.

Top view of dowel-hinged door, showing rounded edge and weatherstrip.

ing the battens, but not the outside corner. Now carve notches in the frame and wall for the pegs at top and bottom, as described for windows and shutters, mount the door, and block off the notches to close them. Finally, along the outside of the hinged edge, attach a strip of rubber or wood all along, to close the crack between door and frame, and attach strips to the frame at the top and other side, with a slab for the sill, as described previously for ordinary doors.

LATCHES

A bar on the inside of the door, running all the way across it, and held in place by two notched pieces of wood attached to the wall at either side, is the easiest way to keep anything or anyone out when you're inside. As for locking the door behind you when you leave, the simplest way is a padlock with hasp or chain. The padlock, however, is obvious evidence to anyone who passes that you are not there. If you are in an area where this knowledge may invite trouble, you may wish to find some less obvious means of locking the door.

Commercial door locks are fairly expensive, and, except in the case of very expensive rustic-looking models, are not at all in keeping with a log cabin. Too, you always have to keep track of your key. The pioneers and Colonials dealt with this problem in various ways, the easiest of which we have used on our two cabins with excellent success. In this method, the principle of the bar is miniaturized, and made to open from the outside when a string is pulled. But the string is carefully concealed, so that you, and any of your friends who know the secret, can open it, but no strangers. It is impossible to tell just by looking whether the owner is at home or not. Of course, you can also just leave the string dangling out when you are only going out to the garden or the like.

Start with any of the doors already described, all finished, hung, and weather-stripped. Carve two notched pieces of wood, each measuring 8 to 10 inches high, at least 2 inches wide, and ¾ to 1 inch thick at the narrowest points. The small flat shelf should be the width of the piece by at least 1 inch deep. Peg, do not nail, one of these to the wall, about 4 inches from the door frame, and in a horizontal line with the other one, pegged to the door itself, about 4 inches in from the edge, and at some point around the middle or upper part of the door which does not interfere with any battens. Use two pegs for each of these, because these provide the strength of the latch. Now take a piece of wood from 12 to 15 inches long, 2 inches wide, and about ⅞ inch thick, for the latch bar. The exact length of it should be enough for it to lie across the two notched pieces with about 2 inches to spare at both ends. Then drill holes in both ends—⅜ inch will do. Fit a loose-headed peg to one end, blind-wedge the peg, and drive the peg into its hole in the wall,

2 inches from the notched piece, with the latch bar still attached loosely to it. The latch bar should now be able to lie across both notched pieces, and swing up out of the way freely.

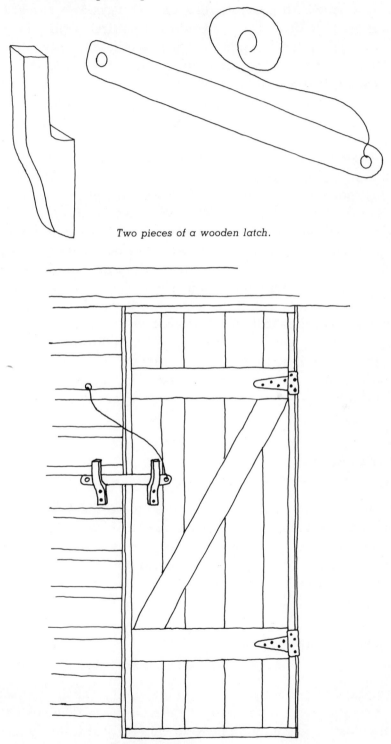

Two pieces of a wooden latch.

The concealed latch in action.

Attach a long string or thin rope to the hole at the latch bar's tip. Nylon or some other nonrotting substance is desirable, though anything will do for a while. Hold the latch bar up vertically, and mark a point on one of the logs a few inches above it. If possible, this should be near a crack, though not so near that the hole drilled there would not be firm. Drill a hole there, all the way through to the outside, large enough to easily put the string through. Make sure your string is long enough to reach from the tip of the latch bar when it is down, up through the hole, and out the other side with at least 6 inches to spare. After putting the string through, tie its end to some small article, such as a 2-inch-long, ¼-inch-thick stick, or a short piece of heavy wire, or the like. This will serve the purpose of a handle, for easy grasping. It remains only to conceal that article. On our cabins, we made the hole through which the string passed ⅝ inch in diameter, so that there was enough space for our little handle to nestle right in it, turned on end, with just its tip protruding a little. Then we smeared a little fresh mud over the hole every time we went out for any length of time, and it was invisible. Positioning the hole very near one of the cracks expedites this, since a little extra mud is less likely to be noticed there than anywhere else.

There are, of course, dozens of other ways to conceal the string pull, and you can no doubt find one that delights you, if you don't care for this one. You can make the whole latch much larger by using the heavy bar, loose-pegged as with the small one, and raising it with a rope instead of a string. Take care to arrange it so that the string lifts up completely out of the way, however. That's an easy mistake to make, and can leave you with a rope barring your entrance even when the door is open.

DOOR HANDLES

Since your door handle does not have to serve the function of latching, you can devise many sorts of attractive ones. A part of a branch where it joins its trunk is good, or an iron ring, such as we found and used on our first cabin, or some magnificent carved piece you devise. This is usually a place where the owner's personality comes to the fore.

SCREEN AND STORM DOORS

These can be made exactly like any of the window sash discussed earlier, although, being larger, they will need extra supports. The easiest way is to use flexible plastic, so you don't have to worry about fitting panes of glass. Or, in the case of a screen door, you can merely nail the screen on with wooden strips. Either a screen door or a storm door should open outward, hinging on the same side as the cabin door, and should be attached at the outer edge of the door frame. If using commercial materials, it is advisable to preserve them in some way, such as with paint, stain, or linseed oil.

DOOR WINDOWS

If your cabin turns out to be a little short on light, you can cut a window in your main door very easily, provided no battens interfere. When cut, nail on flexible plastic with wooden strips both on the inside and on the outside, for an insulated window.

FLOORS

The most obvious floor for a log cabin is dirt, provided the ground is level. A dirt floor, when packed hard by tamping or merely by living, can be surprisingly clean if swept. The Spanish in the Southwest used to treat their dirt floors with coats of bull's blood until they were glossy black and very smooth. If a fire is built in the cabin every day, the floor becomes very dry, and stays dry. And it makes a warm cabin in winter, and a cool one in summer.

The same advantages can be enjoyed with an even cleaner and very durable floor of stone or brick imbedded in the dirt. It is time-consuming, but not difficult, to make, and results in a beautiful, medieval effect. It is our particular favorite.

The pioneers often made floors by simply laying puncheons in the dirt. The puncheons were the full length of the cabin and of a very durable wood, such as white oak. They were carefully settled in, and then trimmed up to level them. Around the fireplace, they were cut away to leave a hearth of dirt for safety.

You can still use any of the above floors even if you have built a good, 12- to 18-inch foundation, by just rolling logs between the foundation points to fill all the gaps, and then chink well. This is good temporarily, if you haven't the time to make a floor on joists, or you can use it forever, by just replacing these logs as they rot.

Making a floor on joists gets you up off the dirt, provides space for storage under the cabin, and makes an easily cleaned floor. To make one, the procedure depends on your materials. With primitive materials, it starts when you lay your sills. At this time, level one pair of sills, the long ones if any, independently, by means of a level, a bowl full of water, or a flat liquor bottle almost full of water. Then lay a hewn slab across from one to the other right in the middle of each, and by adjusting the sills, get them level with one another. When the board is level, the sills will be.

If your cabin is more than 12 feet wide the short way, you'll need a summer beam. This is an 8-inch log, put in at the same time you lay the long sills (or the first two sills, if square), and running the same direction, as an extra support for the floor joists. Support it on its own foundation blocks or rocks, so that it is the same height as the long sills, and exactly in the middle between them.

If by chance you don't read this chapter until too late to put it in this way, you can install the summer beam by rabbet-jointing its two ends so they will sit across two of the midpoint supports on the short walls. And you'll have to prop it up with rocks or blocks along its length too. Be very sure to get its height the same as the long or lower sills.

Lay the second pair of sills, and spike or peg all four corners so the sills and summer beam (if any) cannot creep out of level. Now you're ready for the floor joists. The best solution with primitive materials is round logs with their tops hewn flat. First decide how many you will need, and at what points they should be. With 6-inch logs, make them no more than 3 feet apart. Now mark on your long sills each point for a floor joist. Then take the exact measurement between the center of one sill at the first marked point, and the center of the opposite sill at the corresponding point. Subtract 1 inch from this, and go cut your first joist the resulting length. Hew its top flat, then cut off both its ends at a 45-degree angle, so that the flat side is the longer one. Now lay it in its place, and nail or peg it. In spite of the fact that no two logs are exactly the same thickness, and even the two ends of one log vary widely, the mitered ends will cause them all to level themselves pretty closely without further ado. But be sure to take each measurement carefully, because this will control the possibility of sill logs being bowed here and there. Otherwise they might not all be level.

If you have a summer beam, notch each joist over it before attaching the two ends. And check to make sure that the joist's ends really are sitting down entirely on the two sills, notching deeper over the summer beam if they are not.

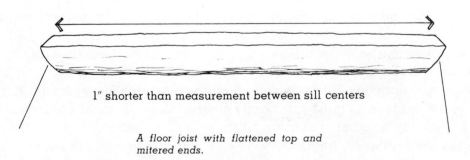

1" shorter than measurement between sill centers

A floor joist with flattened top and mitered ends.

This seems a good time to mention that a level floor is not the necessity it's considered to be, any more than many another modern luxury. Leveling a floor by eye alone will usually yield a product acceptable for living upon, though there may be several inches slope from one end to the other. The body can't always tell the difference if the slope is slight. But for purposes of building in furniture, it becomes more noticeable, and so it is easier to have the floor nearly level, which is why we're going into it. Still, it's not something to worry about.

Now you're ready to lay the flooring, which is best of slabs. Since these are almost certainly green, you shouldn't attach them at all until seasoned. For maximum stability, make them the whole length of your cabin if possible, and just crowd them together tightly and let them lie until next year. As they season, they will shrink in width, so every so often you will have to shove them over and insert another slab to fill the gap. When they are all seasoned, nail or peg them permanently.

You can also make a floor of commercial materials, using two-by-fours or two-by-sixes for the joists, and plywood, ordinary boards or tongue-and-grooved floor boards for the flooring. To do this, level your long sills as before, then attach to them one two-by-four to each, using one nail at the middle of each to start. Then adjust them until level by pivoting them on their nails, and finish nailing firmly with large nails. Now simply lay your joists on end across the two two-by-fours, and nail at each end securely. Space two-by-fours 12 inches apart, and two-by-sixes 18 inches. In the middle of the floor, spike three two-by-fours or two two-by-sixes together and lay them like the others for a middle support. When done, attach your flooring, running perpendicular to the joists where applicable. Whenever boards end, be sure to abut them at a joist.

With any kind of floor, you can double-layer it, for absolute protection from drafts. This is a good idea in colder climates. Just run the second layer of flooring at right angles to the first. Don't do this with a floor of green unattached slabs, however, until the first layer is seasoned and attached.

CHINKING

This is usually the last thing done to the structure itself. It's really very easy, though it can take some time. You can chink with mud, clay, magic cement, Portland cement, or various combinations thereof, with pine pitch, plastic, blood, or other ingredients mixed in. For any chinking mixture, it is best to mix it very stiff, though you may find with some experimentation that a little extra water helps in applying it.

We chinked our first cabin in Kentucky with a mixture of clay and sand

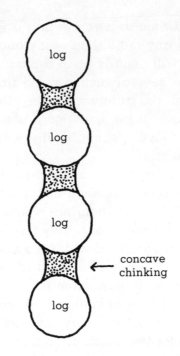

Concave-shaped chinking for maximum durability.

exactly as it came out of the ground, and it set up almost like cement. Not all soils do so well, but we would still recommend anyone who has not built with completely seasoned logs to chink with some primitive mixture the first year at least. The reason is that, as your logs shrink and dry on the wall, whatever you chink with at first is going to crack and fall out anyway, so why waste good cement? After it's seasoned you can use anything you like. But if you're in an area with a good soil type (you can determine this by experimentation), we'd recommend sticking with it. There are many cases of such chinking lasting the life of the cabin.

To help hold the chinking in place to start with, however, you usually have to insert some kind of solid material into the cracks before chinking. This is called caulking, and can be wood strips or thin poles, or nails driven only partly in, so their heads stick out a good bit. Up north it has always been popular to use dried sphagnum moss; of course, other materials can be used. If you disregarded our advice and fitted your logs so closely that the cracks were very small, you will not need caulking. But you will have to chink twice, once inside and once out. Otherwise, chink from inside to get a smoother wall to live with.

After putting wet chinking into a crack, shape it with your hands so it is concave, or curves inward in the middle. This shape has the greatest stability, and also sheds rain best.

8

THE HEART OF THE HOME

Ever since fire was brought successfully inside, it has been the center of domestic activities. The whole family gathered round it at mealtimes, and at every other time possible in cold weather. Naturally, it came to be associated both with warmth and companionship.

The two basic ways of making use of fire are by some type of open fire or a closed stove. Either can be efficient and aesthetic, and both can burn—in addition to wood—coal, peat, or dung.

Fireplaces are beloved by nearly everyone who has ever gazed into the flames and dreamed; they also have their practical advantages. For one, a direct fire is hot as soon as it is lit, unlike a stove, which may take up to half an hour to get hot enough to cook. A fireplace is also quicker to cool after the fire dies down than is a stove. Stoves are more economical and efficient for heating—an advantage in winter, but a disadvantage in summer, when they tend to roast you out. A fireplace, by its very inefficiency, provides much more comfortable summer cooking.

To us, the ideal combination for a permanent home is a fireplace-stove, discussed farther on, plus a small box stove. The stove would handle the bulk of winter heating and cooking, especially *slow* cooking. The fireplace-stove would be used for all cooking during the warm months, and for quick cooking such as breakfast before the stove is hot enough, and it would also be kept going much of the time nine months of the year both for heat and general scenery.

Primitive man, once he had discovered fire, used it outside for a long time. For one thing, he was afraid of it, and wanted to be able to run from it if necessary. For another, he probably experimented with fire in his cave, and found himself smoked out. By the time the American Indians came along, it had been found that if one left a hole in the roof and built the fire underneath, most of the smoke would go out. The Indians were quite stoic about the rest. But most of us today would be dismayed by the amount of smoke left under such circumstances to burn throats and eyes, as a little adjustment is necessary to make primitive methods acceptable to us under any but survival conditions.

THE SMOKE-BACK FIRE

You can build an open fire inside a cabin until you have time for more permanent arrangements if you take care with the fire, keep it away from flammable objects, make a hole in the roof, and provide some incentive to entice the smoke in one direction only—up. The easiest way to do this is the smoke-back fire. Smoke tends to gravitate naturally toward the tallest object around, and to rise upwards along it, if there are no air currents to pull it elsewhere. Ordinarily the tallest object nearby is you, which is one reason many campers have complained of smoke following them. Then, of course, they move to escape it, and the air stirred by their movement creates a partial vacuum, drawing the smoke right after them.

To avoid this problem, erect a light 2- or 3-foot-wide wall of poles behind

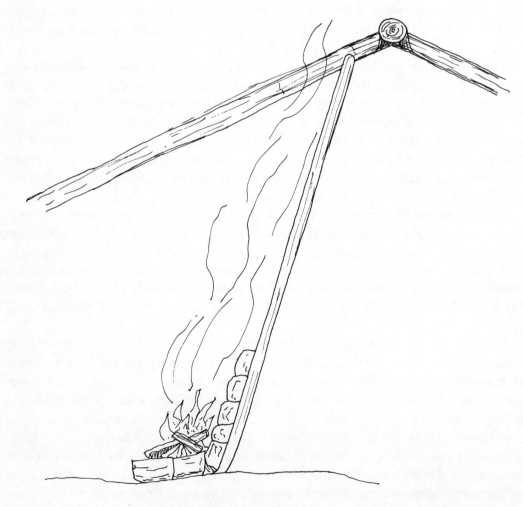

The smoke-back fire.

the fire, tilted slightly backwards, and running up to the hole in the roof. This done, chink the whole thing as well as you can, and line the bottom 3 feet of it with stone or mud brick, or at least plaster very heavily with mud for fire protection. The chinking farther up will prevent the smoke from being drawn through the cracks in to the room behind, instead of going up and out. Be careful to renew the mud plastering at the bottom to prevent any danger of unexpected fire.

When you're finished, the smoke will rise fairly steadily and away from you as you cook or sit by the fire. Because the smoke-back tilts back somewhat, the open hole in the roof is not directly over the fire, so rain is not as likely to interfere. To further deter rain, you can build a bonnet—a small roof on legs—about 1 to 1½ feet above the hole. This will shed rain, yet allow wind to sweep through and pull the smoke out. This will help to prevent down-drafting, too. For more assistance in drawing, you can try opening a window on the opposite side of the cabin facing the fire.

With roofings other than wood, leave the hole vacant as you build. With some wooden roofs, you can cut it out afterwards, then take the pieces you cut out and put them together to make a batten shutter. This can be hinged and closed when desired, although unless you take special pains there will be drips there in hard rains. Slabs attached on end along the uphill and side edges of the hole will serve as gutters and help shed rain away from the opening.

THE CAMP-STOVE FIRE

This arrangement requires more materials and a little more time to make, but it is entirely smokeless. It needs a dirt floor. To make it, dig a 1½-foot-square hole some 4 or 5 feet from a cabin wall. On the side farthest from that wall, dig out a shallow-slanting ramp, instead of a vertical side, down to the bottom of the hole. Then dig a 6-inch-deep trench, running from the hole to the wall, under the wall, and several feet out beyond it. Cover the original hole, not including the ramp, with a metal plate or other suitable cooking surface sturdy enough to hold filled pots for cooking.

At this point you have two choices. For the first, you can lay 6-inch stovepipe in the trench, with an elbow at the point outside the wall where the trench stops, and more pipe rising from there to at least the height of your eaves. Guy the pipe with wire in at least three directions to hold it steady, and cover the pipe in the trench with dirt, both inside and outside the wall, and pat it smooth. Take care to insert a damper in the first section of pipe, about 6 inches beyond the cooktop, for control of heat.

The second choice is to cover the trench with flat rocks, all cracks chinked, up to 6 inches before the trench stops, at which point begin build-

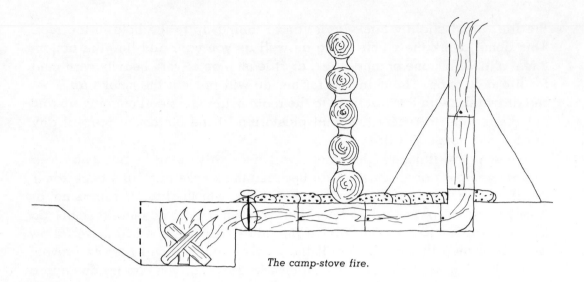

The camp-stove fire.

ing a little straight chimney out of rock or mud brick. Make the inside 6 inches in diameter, and build it at least up to eaves height. With this method, too, a damper will help. You can improvise one by firmly threading a small piece of sheet metal on a piece of heavy wire, so it can be turned to open and close.

Ordinarily, we would not recommend using chinked log cabin construction for anything relating to a fire, but since this little chimney is well outside the wall, and since it is intended as a temporary arrangement, you could use that for the chimney if you are extremely careful in building it (plaster it very well), and in using it (watch it carefully). It might be a good idea to keep a rain barrel standing right next to it, just in case.

To use it, build a fire in the bottom of the hole, and feed it through the ramp. Open the damper wide for maximum draft, and close it for more heat. It should draw excellently, but if not, try a taller chimney or a bonnet.

THE CORNER FIREPLACE

When fireplaces with chimneys were first built, they were simply tapered, with no attempt at controlling the flow of smoke. Such fireplaces are easy to build, and so were often used by pioneers and others in a hurry. But they have the tendency to smoke badly, though those who used them just learned to put up with it. They are also very inefficient at heating, which made them popular in the Colonial South, as it made the kitchens cooler, albeit smoky.

The best intermediate solution we know of between the primitive arrangements (already discussed) and the Rumford-type (covered later) is a corner fireplace adapted from those used by the Spaniards in the Southwest in their adobe houses. To build it, select a corner and make a mark on each wall 5 feet from the corner, near the ground. These marks are shown in the drawing as points B and C, with the corner itself as A. Now, marking on the ground, draw lines BD and CE, each 2½ feet long and each at right angles to its wall. Finally draw a line connecting points D and E. Thoroughly tamp the ground enclosed by your lines to provide a firmer basis for building. It is usual to build a foundation for fireplaces, but since this one is smaller than some, and built entirely indoors, the ground beneath it will not be as subject to changes as outside, and the foundation can be done without.

Line up your building materials. They can be sod, mud bricks (see Rumford-adapted fireplaces for directions in making), magic cement bricks

A corner fireplace.

(made same way), stone, commercial brick, or block. If you can afford commercial materials, you might as well go the whole way and build a Rumford-adapted fireplace. With any materials but sod, you need some kind of mortar, if only mud. Sod doesn't need any because it is a flexible material and fills its own cracks. Sod works well, it's easy to build with, and doesn't burn. Cement, of course, is by far the best mortar, if you can afford it. With commercial brick or block, you'll also need firebrick, both to prevent deterioration of the masonry and to amplify heat. When using firebrick, remember that part of the ultimate thickness of the firebox walls must be allotted to the firebrick, so build your walls thinner accordingly.

Begin building a 1-foot thick wall from B to A to C, up to a height of 40 inches. Then build a 6-inch wall only 1 foot high from B to D to E to C, but leaving 6-inch gaps at points D and E, connecting it at B and C with the thicker wall. Now set 6-inch posts 40 inches high (or 8-inch posts for the heavier building materials) at points D and E, making sure they sit very firmly. These can be logs or can be constructed of your building material, except in the cases of mud brick and sod. If you use logs, sheath them if at all possible with sheet metal, as shiny as possible, if only tin cans cut open and laid flat, nailed on. It will protect the wood from burning by reflecting as much heat as possible back at the fire.

Lay chimney supports horizontally across them, from B to D to E to C. These, too, can be 8-inch logs, with tops flattened and bottoms rabbetted a little so they'll sit firmly on top of the posts. They can also be steel bars or whatever else you can find strong enough to support the entire chimney. Then, lay your pot crane, a length of steel or iron pipe from which you will hang pots on hooks. It should run from F to G, approximately 3½ feet from the corner each way. The pipe should be at least ¾ inch thick.

Begin to build a 6-inch-thick wall on top of the horizontal supports, con-

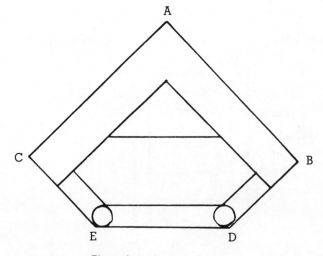

Floor plan of corner fireplace.

necting it with your continuing 1-foot-thick back wall BAC, to form a rough oval. As you build, taper the front and side walls backwards and in toward the center. Make sure that the back wall does not come in to meet them, but continues to lean firmly against the cabin walls, though it, too, will taper sideways. By the time you reach a height of about 76 inches, you should have narrowed it down to a hole diameter of 10 inches, leaning into the corner. Continue the diameter hole from there on up and out. At that point, however, if you wish, you can insert a damper of the same diameter for increased control before continuing to build.

For the best draw, the chimney should stand 3 feet or more taller than the peak of your roof. It should also be on the side of the prevailing wind, which through most of this country is south-west. At least put it at right angles to it, since if it is on the side opposite, eddies are almost certain to prevent drawing and cause down-drafting.

Finally, fill the 1-foot-deep enclosed area at the bottom of your fireplace with dirt, and pack it well until it is flush with the front stone wall. That will be the hearth.

In building fires in it, take care to build them as far back in the corner as possible, burn dry wood, and watch the fire carefully to avoid smoking. Adjusting the damper can help. This done, the fireplace should not smoke much. If it does, you can try some of the techniques listed in the "Trouble-shooting" section of this chapter for the fireplace-stove. But remember that this is not the ultimate in fireplaces. It doesn't take much time, and can't be expected to give excellent results. It's a compromise that may or may not suit your circumstances. You'll have to decide.

This can be converted to a fireplace-stove by inserting into its dirt base a hole covered with a metal cooktop, as described below.

THE FIREPLACE-STOVE

This is an invention of ours that combines all the advantages of a fireplace with some of those of a stove, the additions being primarily for cooking purposes. A box is built into a 1-foot raised hearth, and is covered with a two-piece heavy metal top. Its front can be closed with a hinged metal door, or with an improvised wooden one, spread with an inch-thick layer of mud, then covered with sheet metal.

The box is made about 1½×2 feet, with the wide side turned toward the front. The front piece of the metal top is 1×2 feet, and the back piece is 6 inches by 2 feet.

When a heating fire is built in the fireplace, right on top of the metal plates, cooking can be done by hanging kettles on hooks from the pot-crane. After a couple of hours, baking can be done in the box at the same time; or the box can be used as a warming tray. When you're in a hurry, you can just build a fire in the box itself, remove the narrow back plate to let the smoke escape up and out the chimney, and cook on the front metal plate as you. would on a stove.

This is a much faster way of cooking than building a fire up above, and it's cooler in summer, too. The baking abilities of the box are good, although slow. They can be speeded up, however, by lining the entire box with sheet iron or thin flat stones. The box will also serve as a warm air vent to assist in heating if the door is left open when a heating fire is burning. You can even leave a kettle of water in it to stay hot when you're not using it otherwise.

To build it, you must first start with plans for a functioning fireplace. There's always been a lot of mystery surrounding the building of a fireplace that draws successfully. Count Rumford, in the latter part of the eighteenth century, was the first to study the factors contributing to it, and most good fireplaces since then have employed the principles he came up with. Many books deal with the subject, but it can take a good while to sift through the information and come up with a plan. Here are two that are as likely to work as anything you'll find.

THE FIREPLACE-STOVE

A 36-inch fireplace is the most useful size for one person's cooking and heating. The rest of its dimensions are: height: 28 inches; depth: 18 inches; horizontal back: 22 inches; vertical back: 14 inches; smoke-shelf height: 34 inches; smoke-shelf width: 10 inches; throat depth: 5 inches; smoke-dome height: 18 inches; flue dimensions: 8½×13 inches or 8-inch round.

For a 48-inch fireplace—the most suitable size for two people or more—the dimensions are: height: 33 inches; depth: 19 inches; horizontal back: 33 inches; vertical back: 19 inches; smoke-shelf height: 42 inches; smoke-shelf width: 12 inches; smoke-dome height: 18 inches; flue dimensions: 15 inches round or square.

You must first build a foundation for your fireplace, lest it gradually subside and crumble. You should mark out on the ground the space to be occupied by the fireplace walls, and dig it out to a depth of 2½ to 3 feet, depending on climate, below the ground surface. Then, if you have the materials, fill it with thrown stone, cinders, or a laid foundation, and cover with flat rocks as a building base. If you lack such materials, tamp the bottom of the pit until it compacts no more, then throw in 6 inches of dirt, tamping it also until it will not compact any farther, and keep filling and tamping until the hole is full and solid. Then you may build on it.

If at all possible, build your fireplace within walls, since much less heat is lost and it's less likely to smoke when starting. An inside fireplace will also be more durable, since it isn't subject to the elements. If you haven't room to build it inside, it would be a good idea to build a shed around the back of the fireplace to serve the same purpose and also provide nonfreezing storage. This would also make a good place for animals, if you plan to keep any.

Nowadays, many builders of modern homes surround fireplaces with sunken areas. These provide a cozy relaxation area and also maximize heat from the fire, because warm air rises, and the lower it starts the more area it can warm in passing. Since cold air falls, any cold air in the cabin will be drawn to the lowest area it can find, which will be the sunken area, leaving the other areas warmer. In the sunken area itself, the cold air will be warmed by the fire and sent upward to circulate. So a sunken area is a fine idea if your plans will allow it.

MATERIALS

Commercial materials are easy to work with, and Portland cement holds things together wonderfully. The ideal wall thickness, except in special cases, is 6 inches, but with brick you can get by with 4 inches. These thicknesses may disconcert anyone who is fond of medieval proportions, as we are. Such a wall is not only faster to build and less wasteful of materials, but it also helps the chimney to draw better since it is easier for a fire to raise the temperature of a thin wall to the proper temperature than to do it to a thick wall.

Since you will also have to use firebrick with brick or block, the final thickness will be more than 4 inches. Remember to allot part of the wall's thickness to this, so as not to interfere with the dimensions prescribed.

Stone is also relatively easy to lay with cement for mortar. Here, as with commercial materials, it will help to make a wooden mold to assist in building the inclined surfaces of the back wall and smoke dome.

It is possible to build a stone fireplace without cement mortar. The only difficulties occur at the inclined surfaces. The trick is to inch each layer of rocks out a little farther than the one beneath it on one side, but keep on building the other side up straight. And you must be sure to weight down the other end of each rock that is so protruded, so it can't tip, as you go along. If each individual rock is weighted down, the whole thing will stand. Always offset cracks as much as possible, and lay the stone dry. Though cement is strong enough to hold rocks together solidly, clay and mud are not; to be sure of seating each rock down solidly, you must lay them dry and chink afterwards. Don't wait until the chimney's done, but do 3 feet or so, then chink it, and so on.

The important thing to remember about a stone chimney is that you must have either Portland cement for mortar—or extreme patience. If you are in even a mild hurry and lack cement, you'll do far better to build the somewhat inferior but easy corner fireplace than to try to hurry an uncemented stone Rumford-type. If you hurry, disaster may result.

Mud bricks are an acceptable building material. They are a particularly good material for cold climates, since they are much less conductive than stone. Mud bricks can be produced where many other materials are not available. All soils are not equal in quality for the purpose, but all can be used; it's only a question of durability and relative strength. Of course, if you build inside, this becomes less significant, not only because weather conditions are absent, but because there is frequently a wall to help with support.

The ideal proportions of soil for mud bricks are not less than 50 percent clay and silt and at least 30 percent sand, but you may not be able to obtain such soil. Soil for mud bricks is usually dug from the subsoil, the layer of ground just beneath the topsoil. You can experiment with the subsoil's texture by just taking some in your hands. If it feels gritty, it tends toward sandy, if smooth, more clayey. And if it's about equal, rejoice!

If the soil has too much sand, it won't cohere enough to use. You can test this by making experimental bricks. If it won't work, try digging elsewhere in the same region, preferably in a different sort of location. Within a small radius, acceptable soil can be found in almost any region. If necessary, you can try mixing a small portion of topsoil with it to help it cohere; or dig clay from a river bed and haul it. Straw and other fibrous materials can also be mixed in to help it bond.

The easiest way to make bricks is to use a mold of boards, with sides but no top or bottom. After clearing an area to make bricks on, lay the mold down, fill it with damp mud, mold it firmly into all the corners, and flatten the top. Then immediately pick up the mold, leaving the wet brick there, set the mold down right next to that brick, and make another, and so on. The size bricks used is usually 4 inches tall, 12 inches wide, and 18 inches long.

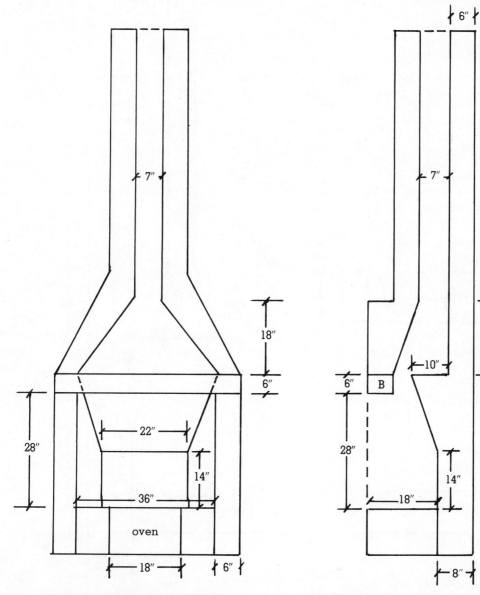

Outline and dimensions of 36-inch-wide fireplace—front.

Outline and dimensions of 36-inch-wide fireplace—side.

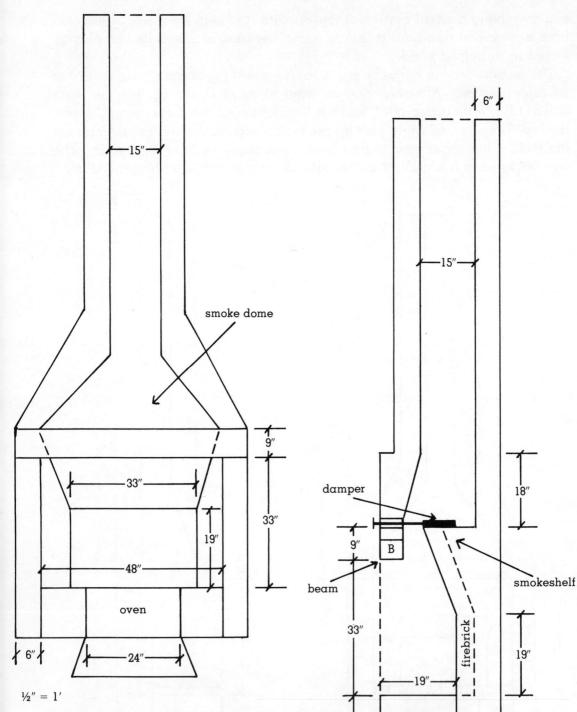

½″ = 1′

*Outline and dimensions of 48-inch-
wide fireplace—front.*

½″ = 1′

*Outline and dimensions of 48-inch-
wide fireplace—side.*

The bricks should be left there to dry about three days before handling, so choose a clear spell. Then they must be stored in a sheltered place for three weeks or more, standing on edge, with air on all sides. When you're ready to build with them, use a mortar made of the same mud, and offset cracks as with brick.

After building a fireplace of these, it is well to plaster it all over on the inside with more mud. Then keep an eye out for cracks as time goes by, and replaster wherever they appear.

Another building material is sod, which was the only one available on the plains. It must be treated with some care, but it's not really flammable, and, like mud bricks, is quite insulative. An inclined back will be difficult to make with it, since it tends to sag, so it might be a good idea to make a small quantity of mud bricks, enough for that one thing only.

WHY NOT LOGS AND MUD?

As you probably know, the pioneers built chimneys of logs and mud, which they called stick-and-daub, so it may occur to you that you could do the same. What is not always considered is how often cabins burned down because of this. It's estimated that nine out of every ten log cabins built burned down at some time, and most of these fires can be attributed to this cause. It is possible to build such a fireplace very carefully, plastering it thickly with mud, and continuing assiduous maintenance on it down the years, never letting wood be exposed to heat. But the likelihood of its turning out that way is slim. It is human nature to grow careless after a time, and as the logs grow ever more seasoned, a slight carelessness may be enough to permit its catching on fire. We strongly urge you to avoid such a chance of disaster, or even tragedy.

BUILDING IT

The actual building is not complicated. Just keep to the dimensions shown as carefully as possible. Above a certain height, you will have difficulty in lifting your rocks or bricks, so you can build some sort of scaffolding platform. In doing this, make use of any little hills that rise near your cabin walls for one end of the scaffolding's support. Provided you're building the chimney outside, you could pile up a dirt mound for the same purpose, or you can attach part of it to any handy tree or stump. If you're building inside, you may be able to employ the cracks in the walls. And, of course, you can make it free-standing, with a ladder up to it.

At the proper height, lay a metal pole across the width, about halfway back, for your pot-crane. The right height for this is the same as the bottom of the lintel, or support beam, which runs across the front of the fireplace opening to hold the front masonry wall.

For the lintel itself, use a log at least 8 inches in diameter with its top flattened. This is what was usually used in the past. However, this gradually becomes somewhat charred, and can constitute a fire hazard if not kept carefully smeared with mud. It's a good idea to sheath it with sheet metal, such as tin cans nailed on, with a layer of mud between the metal and the wood for insulation.

You can also use steel bars for the lintel, or a concrete beam cast in place. If you can find a suitable length of old railroad rail, that would last forever.

When you've completed the smoke shelf, it's time to put in the damper if you're going to have one. If the throat is made as narrow as recommended, you don't really need a damper, but it's a good thing to have all the same. It won't assist the draw except occasionally, but it will prevent cold air from entering when the fire's not lit, and will keep out insects, snakes, and mice.

The simplest damper is a sheet of heavy iron or steel, the same length as the throat, and slightly wider, with two rigid rods attached. These rods must be long enough to reach from the edge of the smoke shelf straight through two small holes left in the front wall at the same height. By pushing or pulling the rods, you can close or open the damper. Be sure to build the damper in now, since you won't be able to put it in afterwards.

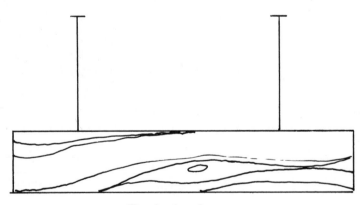

The simplest damper.

Tapering the smoke dome is fairly easy. You can use a wooden mold with commercial materials and cement, but it's better not to otherwise, since you need to keep tabs on the strength and balance of the masonry as you build with other materials. Just keep edging it in as with the inclined back. If it doesn't reach the proper flue size at the right height, it's not as important here as for the inclined back. Keep tapering it in until it's right.

If you're building with commercial materials, you need clay flue lining for the flue if your walls are less than 8 inches thick. Otherwise, it is unnecessary.

To prevent your roof from leaking where the chimney emerges, you'll have to flash, or seal, around it. Flexible metal is the most convenient material for this if you can buy or scavenge it. Cut-up tin cans will do if you're careful to paint with pine pitch, melted plastic, or roofing cement. When your chimney is exactly the same height as your roof, build pieces of sheet metal into it, one edge sticking into the masonry, the other overhanging and covering the hole surrounding the chimney. These should each overlap the next, all the way around the chimney, and should then be attached firmly. Finally, coat the whole thing with whatever goop you are using to seal out rain.

You can also flash with wood, by nailing together very shallow V-troughs and inserting one end into the masonry while building, so that that end overlaps the other end of the V, and sheds. But coat it carefully. Metal is better, if you can get it.

BUILDING WITH A COMMERCIAL FORM

This is certainly the easiest way to obtain a fireplace, though they frequently do not draw any better than those built without. It is also expensive, with the average form costing $200 or more. The best known domestic brands are Majestic, Heatform, and Heat-a-lator. More expensive yet, and also more advanced, are various Scandinavian brands, which are very heavily made, with beautiful decorations. The best-known brand in the United States is Jøtul.

Building with a commercial form is much the same as building without, except that there is no difficulty about inclining surfaces, since that is molded into the form.

TROUBLESHOOTING

If you built the fireplace as described and still have trouble with smoking and down-drafting, the chances are that one or more of the following things is at fault:

- The chimney is too low. It should go up to 3 feet above the peak of the roof.
- There is a hill or ridge near your cabin, causing a wind eddy, which prevents it from drawing as it should.
- The smoke shelf may be too narrow for your particular conditions. Try artificially widening it by closing the damper an inch or so.
- The front of the opening may be too high for your situation. Build up the hearth a couple of inches with dirt or stone to raise the fire height. Or

try a grate or andirons, either the regular sort or improvised with two rows of rocks across which the logs are laid.

- If you're burning green wood, you may not have sufficient draft for it to burn smokelessly. Make sure the damper is open all the way, or try opening a window on the opposite side of the cabin.
- The fire may be improperly laid. A sideview of your fire ought to show the line of wood slanting up toward the back, not otherwise.
- It will draw better if the very top of the chimney is made with the tops of the walls slanting up toward the center.
- It can be made to draw better by constricting the flue size a couple of inches for a foot or so at the top of the chimney. This can be done while building if you have doubts about the ability to draw, or you can add on an extra foot later with the smaller diameter. This helps by speeding up the flow of smoke and gasses at the point of emergence, which tends to shove aside downdrafts.
- A bonnet can help. This can be made of sheet metal in a slightly conical shape, and should be punctured in several places to prevent its holding a pocket of water. This shape tends to repel downdrafts without restricting the rising of smoke and warm gasses. You can also improvise a bonnet from one of the round aluminum sleds children play with. Beat it gently with a hammer to make it more conical and less rounded, punch or bore holes, and proceed.

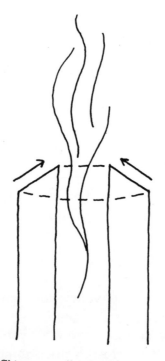

Chimney walls slanting up toward center to improve draw.

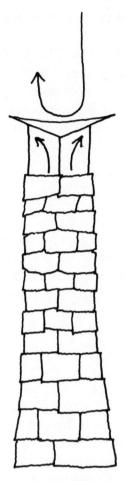

An improved bonnet.

ACCESSORIES

Poker and tongs are necessary around any fire. They can be made of wood, replaced every so often. Let the poker be at least 2 inches thick, with a notch near its far end, and you can use it to lift pots off their hooks over the fire.

For hanging pots from the pot-crane, you need pothooks. Unless you can obtain old ones used for the purpose, or more recent ones made for hanging a side of beef, your best bet will be to get several assorted lengths of strong chain and eight or ten sturdy S-hooks. Wrap the chains at points along the pot-crane, and adjust the position of the S-hooks as desired to regulate the height (and therefore the heat) at which the pots hang. Of course, this requires pots with bails.

Grates are not necessary, but there is one we've seen that increases the fire's heating capacity by drawing cold air in through tubes and, after heating it, lets it pass out into the room again. It's very efficient, if not exactly lovely.

Those who have children may find it highly desirable to have a fire screen. We would certainly recommend it. But otherwise, it isn't necessary, if you're careful. Never leave the room with a fire going, and provide a suitably deep hearth, a minimum of 18 inches deep by the width of the firebox, of nonflammable material such as dirt or masonry.

STOVES

Because of the recent upsurge in interest in wood heat, due to the unusual weather patterns and the energy crisis, many companies that had virtually discontinued production have now resumed making wood stoves. These come in numerous sizes and shapes for different purposes.

COOKSTOVES

At the top of the line as far as size and luxury go is the Queen Atlantic type. This particular model is made by the Portland Stove Foundry of Portland, Maine, and features six cooktops, a spacious oven, two warming trays, a water reservoir, and beautiful original Victorian styling, in heavy cast iron, for some $800. It will cook for an army, and was a standard on many working farms a hundred years ago. It's worth every penny if you have a big family.

There are also smaller cookstoves, with four cooktops, oven, and with or without reservoirs and warming trays. Some of them come in porcelain enameling, which is supposed to stay cleaner-looking. Presumably they hold up, though our experience in general with porcelain enamel, admittedly not on stoves, has been that it always chips after a while.

Fisher stoves employ sophisticated principles for maximizing economy of fuel, and are also usable for cooking, though without cooktops. At least two of their models have dual top surfaces, at different heights, to provide two different cooking temperatures. They are considered excellent, but are also rather expensive.

In the same category are various brands of European stoves; Jøtul is the best-known brand in this country. They are beautiful stoves, of the heaviest cast iron, and very efficiently engineered for economy. They, too, can be used for cooking, but are also expensive. Their smallest model sells for about $250.

*A small Lange stove from Denmark.
It sells for about $275.*

*A large old-fashioned type of heat-
ing stove, with porcelain-enamelled
shell.*

At the inexpensive and small end of the list is a type made by most American manufacturers, the two-cooktop box stove, which has quite a history. It's been commonly used all over America in the last hundred years, especially on the frontiers, because it is small, yet puts out a great amount of heat and can be cooked on very satisfactorily.

They sell new, on the average, for $100 to $150. Montgomery Ward, L. L. Bean, and numerous hardware stores have them. We got ours used. It had a crack, and the seams needed sealing, but otherwise it was intact, and we paid $25. It is the sole heating and cooking device in our Wisconsin cabin and in the hard winter of 1976-77 heated our tent. It is a champion.

A used stove is an excellent idea if you're short on money. Just watch carefully, and examine the merchandise for cracks, missing equipment, and broken bolts or fittings. Cracks can usually be fixed with furnace cement, sold in hardware stores, and broken bolts can be replaced, but missing cooktops or legs can be quite a problem, so beware.

This type of stove is ideal for one or two people in a small cabin, or in combination with the fireplace-stove in a larger cabin. It's the best combination of cheap and versatile we've found.

HEATING STOVES

This category of stoves is made for heat only. Because of their various constructions, it's hard to cook effectively on them, though you can eventually boil a teakettle.

The smallest is a tiny potbellied stove. It gives out a surprising amount of heat for the wood it burns, and takes up comparatively little space. And it is possible to do a little cooking on its one cooktop. It's fairly inexpensive, from $50 to $65.

For about the same price you can buy a sheet-metal version of the box stove. Unlike the iron version, it has no cooktops and will hardly even boil a teakettle, but it gives out a lot of heat. Due to its thinner metal, it won't hold its heat as long as cast iron, but then it's also much cheaper.

A third type is the Ashley Thermostatic Heater, and similar models. It's an ugly, graceless cylinder, but it is economical of wood, and a good heater.

Another, older type, shaped somewhat like a potbellied stove, is of very heavy cast iron underneath and is surrounded with a porcelain enameled shell, which is designed to circulate warm air evenly throughout a large area. Again, cooking is all but impossible.

Finally, there is the Franklin stove. It was designed by Benjamin Franklin to be a free-standing iron fireplace, with doors that could convert it to a box stove. These are very popular today, since they allow the enjoyment of a

A Franklin stove.

fireplace without troublesome installation. They don't give as much heat as most stoves, and do not have a fireplace's cooking potential, unless you hang a pot down inside, but they have a very nice effect, and will help with heating. Prices run from $150 to $300.

HOMEMADE STOVES

If some of the above prices leave you dazed, and you can't locate a suitable used stove, you can build your own. The quickest ones can be made from a 55-gallon drum. There are kits you can order, from L. L. Bean for one, which include an iron door, legs, and pipe collar, for converting such a drum. Bean's kit sells for $55.

Most people just use the drum in the round as a heating stove only, but if you cut a slit down the side from top to bottom, disconnect about 1½ feet of metal adjoining the slit, and flatten out the resulting flap of metal, you can reattach the edge of the flap and have a flat cooking surface.

Another way is to cut the whole drum in half, from top to bottom, not through the middle. Attach legs to the bottom, and 1½-foot supports from its corners to support the top half. Cut a hole in the top half to fit the stovepipe, and lay heavy screen or iron grid over the bottom half, unattached. Then

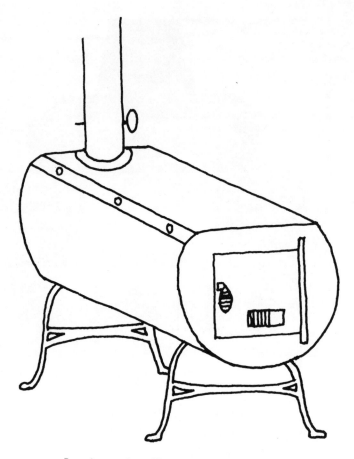

*Barrel stove from 55-gallon drum. Top
flattened for cooking.*

you can remove the screen or grid, build a fire, and replace the screen as
a cooking surface. The top will serve as a hood to take all the smoke out.
A layer of sand in the bottom will help it last longer.

We have seen stainless steel 55-gallon drums advertised for sale cheap.
If you used one of these you would really have a superior and permanent
product, whichever way you made it.

With any stove, you need a nonflammable surface for it to stand on. This
can be dirt, rock, brick, or commercially made metal-covered asbestos pads.
Remember never to locate a stove nearer than 18 inches to any flammable
surface or object. With stoves of thinner metals than cast iron, the distance
should be increased to a very minimum of 2 feet for safety.

There are other more aesthetic and permanent ways to build stoves, too.
If you know how to work metal, you can make your own metal one for a frac-
tion of the cost of buying one, and with features designed to suit your needs.

You can also make one out of stone, brick, or mud brick. In essence, all
it need be is a box about 2½ feet tall, filled with dirt or similar material up

to about a foot below the top. A metal plate is laid over the top, except for 6 inches at one end, where the stovepipe will be, and a 1-foot square door on the opposite end, which you left open in building for the purpose.

Iron or steel is best for the door, welded if possible to a rod that will provide a dowel hinge along the top edge of the door. If this is beyond you, a wooden door can be used, held in place only by friction, with its inside first thickly plastered with mud, then covered with sheet metal nailed on.

The stovetop, too, should be of heavy gauge metal, if possible, although thin metal can be used if adequately supported and replaced from time to time. You can even use a flat rock for the cooktop if you can find the right kind, but that can be difficult. It has to be of uniform thickness, 1 inch to 1½ inches, of a hard, nonabsorbant rock type, and can't be found anywhere near a creek or river bed or lakeshore, since those rocks nearly always have moisture trapped inside, which when heated turns to steam and explodes the rock. If you find the perfect rock, support it with rods or pipe, and it will be excellent, slower-heating than iron, but staying hot longer.

Finally, you need a chimney and damper. The chimney can be of stovepipe, or of whatever the rest is built of. In whichever case, start laying

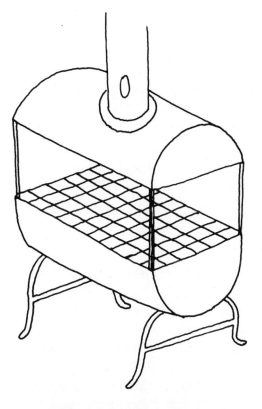

Barrel stove made by cutting 55-gallon drum in half, using bottom for cooking surface and top for hood.

A homemade stone stove.

around the open 6-inch strip at the back of the stovetop, gradually narrow-ing the opening to about 6-inch round, at about 1 foot above the stovetop height. At this point, put in your damper, which can be bought for the pur-pose or a makeshift job. If you make your own, make it a heavy job, since you won't be able to replace it if it burns out without tearing down the whole chimney.

If you're going to use stovepipe, this is the place to start with it, fitting its bottom edge very firmly into the 6-inch hole, and building the masonry up around it another 6 inches to hold it solidly. If building with masonry, just continue the 6-inch hole straight on up and out through the roof. A masonry chimney will need no care as to protecting the wood it may pass near, but with stovepipe you'll have to take great pains to prevent a fire hazard. You should make your holes in ceiling and roof at least 6 inches larger on all sides than the stovepipe, and flash them well.

Last, seal around the edges of the stovetop with mud to prevent smoke from escaping into the room there.

A mud brick stove will give out heat only through the cooktop. This is excellent for cooking, but not so good for heating, which would commend this stove for use in warm climates. For colder climates, however, you would probably have to combine it with a fireplace to get sufficient heat.

HINTS ON COOKING

Fireplaces are quite different from stoves when it comes to cooking. Each has its tricks that can take you a good while to learn, as it did us, so we'll give you a few to start with.

When cooking at a fireplace, whether with the fireplace-stove or otherwise, you have to adapt yourself to the fire or waste fuel and time. A fire is hottest right after it's first started, so this is the time to boil water for coffee, tea, or other purposes. After this initial stage of extreme heat, which lasts for up to ten minutes, there is the stage of moderate to high heat, which can be sustained for as long as you keep the fire built up. This is the time to do most cooking, other than frying or broiling, such as boiling pota-

FIREPLACE COOKING PARAPHERNALIA

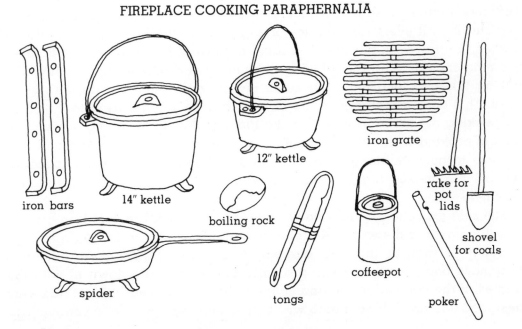

iron bars   14" kettle   boiling rock   12" kettle   iron grate   rake for pot lids   shovel for coals

spider   tongs   coffeepot   poker

Fireplace or stove cooking paraphernalia.

toes, cooking vegetables, and the like. When you cease to build up the fire, it will subside after a while to a low flame, which may last up to half an hour. This is good for simmering and frying. Finally it will die down to coals, which are perfect for low-temperature frying, broiling, and toasting.

One way to get around this sequence if necessary is to steam many items that you might otherwise fry or toast, such as bread. By doing this you can make use of the hottest flames or the moderate ones without danger of burning.

A stove is entirely different. When you start the stove, especially with green wood, build it up high and leave the draft and damper wide open for ten to fifteen minutes to get a roaring fire. Then close it halfway for another ten minutes, and finally shut it down almost completely. By then it should be plenty hot for cooking. Any time you add fresh fuel, open it up at least halfway, maybe more, depending on how dry and how large your fuel is. Give it ten or fifteen minutes before shutting down again. But always remember to close it, or all your heat will go out, instead of getting the stove hot enough to cook or heat.

Unless you have a stove with an oven, you need some means of baking. The best way to solve this problem is baking with coals in a cast iron dutch oven. The dutch oven is a comparatively shallow kettle with three legs and a lid that is flanged for the purpose of holding coals on it. When you want to bake, preheat both kettle and lid (lid upside down) on your fire or stove, put the food inside, either directly on the bottom or in another pan, clap on the lid, and cover the lid with coals from the fire. It takes a good many coals, and to get them at exactly the right stage you'll have to build a fire forty-five minutes or so in advance. Set the kettle in a safe, windless place, and check on it every ten minutes or so by lifting the lid carefully, with its coals still on it, with the tine of a rake, a piece of heavy wire, or whatever is strong enough to lift the lid without bending or dropping it. If what you're baking takes so long that your coals die on you, replace them with fresh ones. This does a really good job of baking once you get used to it.

Speaking of cast iron, it is also the ideal cookware for doing every other kind of cooking with either a fireplace or a stove. Once it is seasoned, it is difficult to burn anything, and its even distribution of heat yields superior results and makes the best use of whatever temperature your fire has reached.

The sole exception to the rule is water-boiling, because cast iron gives a metallic flavor to the water. Aluminum, stainless steel, or porcelain enamel is better for that. By the way, one way to boil water quickly on a stove is to remove one pot lid and slip the coffeepot or teakettle down in with the flames, if the pot is of a size and shape to fit. This is what the pot lids were designed for, since direct flame will boil something faster than conduction.

9

FINISHING UP

Now that the shell of your cabin is done, and you have arranged for your means of cooking and heating, you can attend to furnishing the cabin. Furniture is not actually a necessity, but a certain amount of the right furnishings can do much to provide convenience in living, and your cabin should have been planned with those in mind.

It is possible to buy part of the furnishings. Tables and chairs or benches, easy chairs, and the like are fairly common and will probably fit in the space you have unless you have built a very tiny cabin. Less expensive are many items made especially for family campers, among them a rather nice-looking and sturdy folding table with attached benches to seat four people. Probably the most worthwhile article to buy is a folding canvas easy chair, since easy chairs are a little more trouble to build than most furniture. These come in many versions. A small one of aluminum tubing sold by L. L. Bean for $8 has proved very satisfactory to us after three years of constant use as our only easy chair. For even greater relaxing luxury, there is a similar but larger chair made by LaFuma, which sells for about $25.

Often it is possible to salvage the frames of aluminum folding chairs from dumps, and reweb them for use. But all the furniture necessary for your cabin can be made very sturdily and beautifully from natural materials, and these are really the most appropriate of all. Even if you buy some items, you'll have to build others, such as pantries, since they won't be available otherwise. Nails are not even necessary for most pieces, although they can certainly help to speed up the building process.

CHAIRS

The simplest form of chair is a stool with no back. The easiest way to make one of these is to cut a log section 18 inches high and 12 to 18 inches through, remove the bark, stand it on end, and sit on it. But it does require sawn ends.

If you lack the saw, you can take the same size log section, with chopped ends, and merely lay it down and sit on it. But it will tend to roll, of course, as well as being rather bumpy to sit on. Two more steps will solve this. First, find two 18-inch sections of a much smaller log, say 6 inches through, and notch the underside of your thick log twice so that it will sit across both smaller ones. It won't roll any more. Then hew the top surface flat to remove the bumps. If you don't have any 12- to 18-inch logs, you can make the same stool by splitting a 6- to 9-inch log in half, smoothing both flat surfaces, and notching their undersides over the two small log sections. This stool is very primitive, of course, but will give you a place to sit within fifteen minutes, and you can replace it later if you like.

A third type of stool is a little more complicated. You need either a puncheon or a 3- to 4-inch-thick slab, 18 inches long and at least 12 inches wide. Bore four holes into the underside, about 1½ inches in diameter and 1 to 2 inches deep. Cut four pole sections about 16 inches long and a little thicker than your holes. Whittle the ends to achieve a perfect, very snug fit, so tight that you have to beat them a little to fit them in. Then stand the stool up and cautiously adjust the length of the legs, if necessary, to make it stand approximately level. Don't be too greedy! (Making legs the same length is every amateur carpenter's eternal bugaboo, so watch out. Many have lost a seat but gained a footrest.)

If you build this stool with green wood, the legs are going to shrink as they dry out, and will loosen and fall out of their holes. Don't worry about this; just fit blind wedges when it occurs. To do this, saw or cut with your knife a narrow slot in the top of each leg, maybe ¼ inch thick and 1 inch

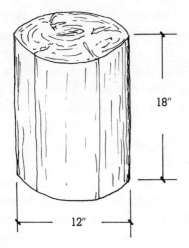

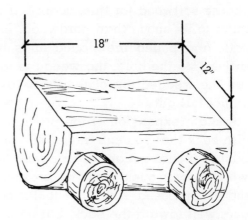

A simple stool made from a section of log.

A stool requiring no sawing.

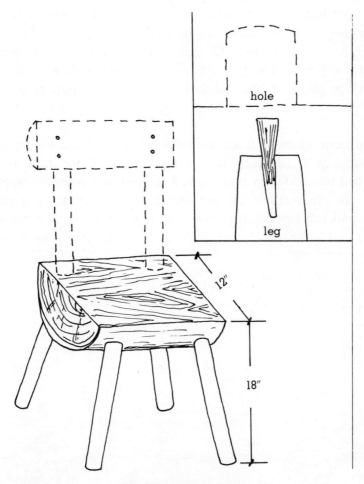

Puncheon stool with legs. Closeup of blind-wedging procedure.

deep. Then make four wedges a little longer and thicker than the slots. Choose softwood for this, seasoned if at all possible, since it will conform better to its space than hardwood. Insert all the wedges partially into their slots, and pound the slotted ends into the holes. As each leg is pushed farther into the hole, the wedge is forced deeper into the slot. The result is that the wedged top of the leg is actually thicker than the hole, and thus cannot fall out.

A slight expansion of the previous stool will give you the simplest chair with back that you can make. The only difficulty is that the seat must be at least 18 inches square. If you don't have that size log, you can put together two narrower ones with two cross-supports pegged or nailed underneath, and then proceed. After the stool is completed, bore two holes in the top surface, well toward the back, but no nearer than 1½ inches to the edge. Slant your holes back slightly so that the top is 1½ inches from the back edge, but the bottom of the hole is farther from it. Then get two pole sections 1½ inches thick and 15 to 18 inches long, and whittle their ends as before to ensure a perfect fit, but do not insert them yet. First prepare their ends with blind wedges right from the start, so there'll be no surprises later on. Now take a small slab or puncheon 18 inches long and about 6 inches wide, make two shallow notches on its back at the proper points to cradle the two poles, and nail or peg it to the poles at the notches. Finally, put the whole backrest into position and pound it in. This is a good chair for sitting at a table.

The same principle can be used to make a longer bench for more than one person to sit on just by making the seat and back longer, and, if the length desired is over 3 feet, adding two more legs and one more backrest support in the middle. To make this more comfortable for relaxing, you can also tilt both the seat and the backrest a little, by mounting the seat on the legs at

Sawless stool expanded into a bench.

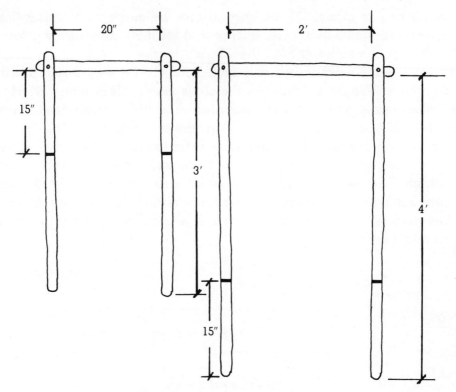

The two frames put together for an easy chair.

a slight angle. (If you want a bench longer than 3 feet, it's best to use slabs for both seat and backrest, since obtaining puncheons longer than 3 feet causes new problems.)

An easier bench is made by extending the length of the second type of stool mentioned previously. This has a way of looking even nicer as a bench than as a stool. With a massive seat-log, you could attach a back as described above, but otherwise it isn't practical.

Relaxing chairs usually take more time to construct, but this one is still not difficult. It is made like a typical canvas folding chair, with canvas, leather, or whatever for the seat. First provide two 4-foot poles, 2 inches thick, two 3-foot poles the same thickness, one 2-foot pole, and one 20-inch pole, each also 2 inches thick. You will need a piece of canvas or similar material, at least 4½ feet long and 18 inches wide. And a few nails will facilitate things, though they aren't absolutely necessary.

To begin, measure 15 inches from one end of each of the 3-foot and 4-foot pieces, and mark all. You're going to build two 3-sided frames, one larger than the other. The larger will use the two 4-foot poles and the 2-foot pole. To join them, notch the two 4-foot poles over the 2-foot pole. Make the notches in the 4-foot poles at the ends opposite from the 15-inch marks you made, and make your joint at the very ends of the poles. Fit them together and nail or peg in place. Do the second one the same way, using the two 3-foot poles and the 20-inch pole, except that for this one, put the crosspiece and notches at the same end as the 15-inch marks.

At each of those marks, drill a ½-inch hole all the way through horizontally, running the same direction as the crosspieces. Make every effort to get these holes really straight and parallel with the crosspieces, and not slanted a little one way or another. When the four holes are drilled, whittle two pegs with heads on them, just a little thinner than ½ inch but not as thin as ⅜ inch. The pegs should be 5 inches long, and the head 1 inch wide and ½ inch thick. Test them in the holes to make sure they fit loosely. A little linseed oil wouldn't hurt on them, for extra lubrication. Whittle two round little caps identical to the peg heads, and drill a ⅜-inch hole exactly in the center of each, ¼ inch deep.

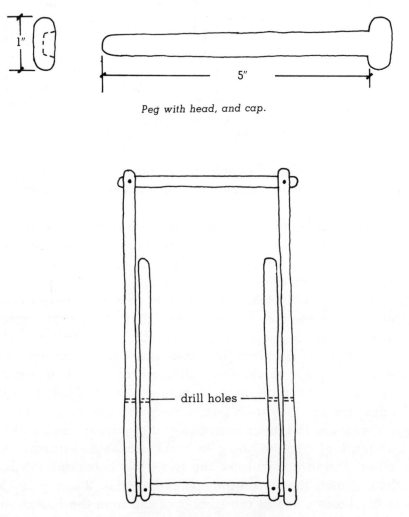

Peg with head, and cap.

Frames lined up for pegging.

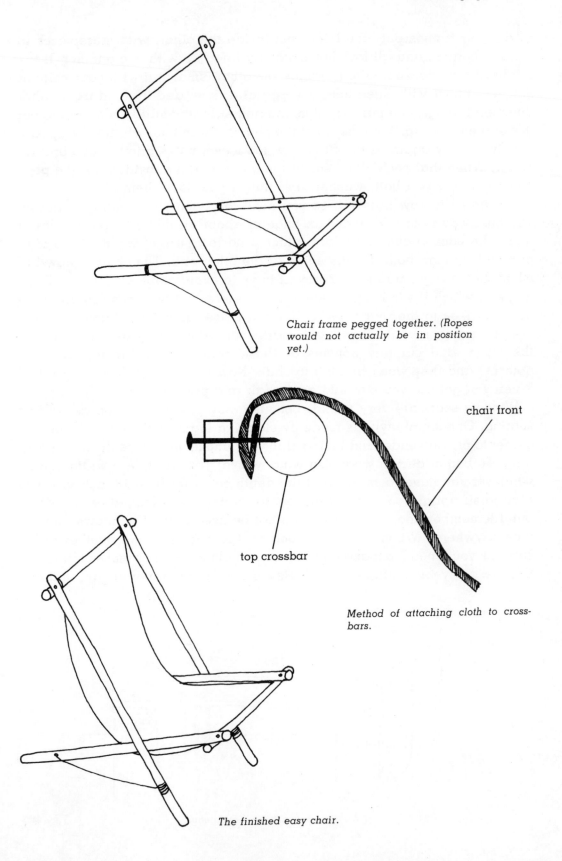

Chair frame pegged together. (Ropes would not actually be in position yet.)

chair front

top crossbar

Method of attaching cloth to crossbars.

The finished easy chair.

Lay your frames out, one lying just inside the other, with crosspieces at top and bottom, and all four holes exactly lined up with one another. If the smaller frame doesn't quite fit inside the other, smooth it with your knife or hatchet until it will. Then take one peg at a time, and insert it from either direction through one pair of holes, making sure it is still loose. Try to beat one of the little caps onto the tip of the peg. If it won't go, whittle it very cautiously and try again. If the fit is now too loose, make another cap and try again. When that peg's finished, fit the other one. A substitute for the pegs and caps here is a bolt, washer, and nut, if you have them.

The frame is now finished, so you need to attach your seating material. The best way is to fold under an edge of about an inch at one end, lay it along the back of one crosspiece, place a narrow strip of wood on top of it, and nail through both. Do the same at the other end. The chair is now finished, but it won't stand up. You will have to experiment with it to find the angle at which it sits best, or which you prefer. First tie ropes running from the front legs to the rear ones. By sliding these around you can determine the position you want. Then make marks where the ropes are tied, remove the ropes, and cut tiny notches at those points. Retie the ropes in the notches, and they won't be able to slide. Now you can sit down and relax! When you get up, you can fold your chair and put it away.

Window seats are very useful, because they provide storage as well as seating. One simple type is made by standing log sections on end close together to provide ends, and laying slabs or puncheons across them and pegging. To begin, decide what size window seat you want. The width can be whatever you have room for, and the depth can vary from 18 inches, if you plan to sit upright on it, to 30 inches, for sitting cross-legged or sprawling out. (Remember, too, that these need not be used only at windows, but are nice anywhere.) When you've decided on the size, saw the number of log sections you'll need to make up both ends, making them 18 inches minus the thickness of your seating material. Hew slabs of the proper length, and pre-

Window-seat with log-section ends.

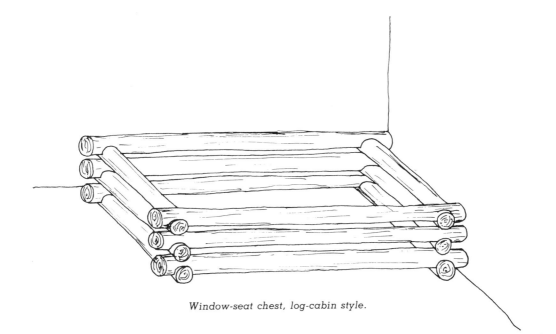

Window-seat chest, log-cabin style.

pare enough pegs to put one into each end of each slab. Collect all your
materials at the spot where you intend the window seat to stand, since,
once built, it is not very portable. Stand up your log sections where they be-
long, and play with them to get them all to stand properly. If your log sections are thicker than 6 inches, you'll probably need nothing more than
we've mentioned so far, since their weight and bulk will give sufficient stability. With smaller logs, it's a good idea to hew two more slabs, of the
seat's depth, and peg them along the tops of the log sections first. Then lay
your slabs across and peg or nail; otherwise, you can just peg the slabs directly to the log sections.

This design is open to much variation. For example, the ends may be built
out of stone or brick, and the seat may be of poles thickly coated with magic
cement, for a smooth surface. And, of course, you can use two-by-fours or
plywood, too. One note, though: if the width will be over 4 feet, put an extra
row of supports in the middle.

The storage underneath can be used for a woodpile, which is very picturesque, or any number of things. If what you plan to store isn't very pretty,
you can conceal it by closing in the front with log sections just like the ends,
and having the seat lift instead of being pegged down. Or you can hang a
cloth curtain down from the seat, or you can build it completely concealed
to start with.

This completely enclosed window seat is really more like a chest. As the
drawing shows, it is made by simply notching poles in the same way as
when you built the cabin. If you plan to store cloth or paper goods in this,

and can find cedar poles to use, so much the better. The top can be made like a batten door, or in any other way, just so it is liftable. You can use hinges or not, as you wish.

BEDS

First of all, beds can be made by expanding the size of any of the window seats discussed above, and will provide a lot of storage underneath.

If you're short on space, you can make a folding bed by merely attaching a batten doorlike platform the correct size for you to two ropes running to the wall. One edge would also be hinged to the wall. It's a good idea to make a little rim of poles 1 to 2 inches high all around the bed's edges to prevent your falling out of bed and to help keep bedding in place when you fold the bed up.

You can build the following type of bed either for use as a trundle bed, stored during the daytime underneath another larger bed, or simply for use as a permanent fixture if you have plenty of space. First, cut four 6-inch log sections, two long enough for your desired bed length plus an 18-inch allowance for the corner joints, and two the right width plus 18-inch corner allowance. (For a trundle bed, which will have to be moved twice a day, better use 4-inch poles with 12-inch allowances.) Before building it as a permanent bed, drag all the pieces to the spot, and build it in place.

Notch the two short logs over the two long ones, leaving overhangs of half the logs' thickness beyond each notch, and nail or peg each notch firmly. Make enough slabs or puncheons of the necessary width to fill the space, taking care to make them as uniform as possible; the more even the surface is, the better you'll sleep. When they're all ready, lay them across and nail if you have nails. If using slabs, flatten the surfaces of the long logs a little by hewing slightly, so the slabs will sit smoothly. If using puncheons, notch the undersides a little so they'll rest firmly, and adjust for a smooth surface by the same means. You can also use boards, two-by-four's, plywood, or particle board for this, if thick enough for good support. If necessary, you can also run a third log down the middle.

If using pegs, take a pair of 2-inch poles the same length as the bed, and cut off their ends at a slant so that they will lie right down on the slabs, puncheons, etc. Holding them down as flush as possible, directly on top of the original long logs, peg through their points into the head and foot logs. Then put one peg through at the middle of the pole, down into the long log. Take care that the pole presses down as much as possible on the bed-boarding because that is what holds the boards in place without each one being pegged.

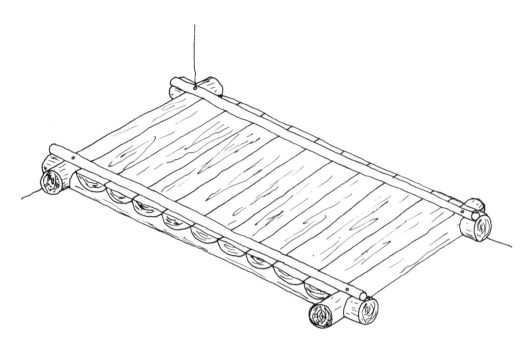

Permanent or trundle bed.

With the same four-log frame described above, you can take strips of rubber tire, and weaving them back and forth in 4-inch squares, produce a springy and very durable bed. To obtain the strips, cut them longitudinally from the road surfaces of tires, checking to make sure none of them are damaged. You can use a hacksaw or tinsnips for this, but either way it will take some time. Then attach all the vertical strips first by nailing, and follow by nailing each horizontal at one end, and weaving it under and over the verticals, before pulling tight and nailing at the other end. The same process can be used with leather or rope, except that the squares should be made smaller, and in the case of rope, the rope should be tied to or wound around thick driven nails instead of being nailed down.

A bed can be made standing up, with space underneath like conventional ones, by simply raising up the whole frame on four 9-inch log sections (sawn ends) 18 inches high, and pegging. Again, build on the spot.

To build a bed off the ground in a corner, start by measuring up from the floor in that corner to the bottom of the first crack which is at a convenient height for your bed. Then saw a log section that fits that measurement, of hardwood if possible, and at least 9 inches thick. While you're at it, get two 6-inch logs, one the desired length of your bed plus 9 inches, and the other the desired width plus 9 inches. With your axe or hatchet, chop a point on the end of each of these last two, and take all three back to the corner. By experimenting with the two 6-inch logs, ascertain where the outside corner of your bed will be, and place the 9-inch log section there. With their straight-sawn ends resting on the 9-inch log, fit the pointed ends of the 6-

inch logs into their respective cracks in the wall, and notch the one that is higher over the other one at the 9-inch log, leaving a 3-inch overhang. (Yes, one will be higher than the other because one crack will be higher.) From there, fill it in by any of the methods already described. If you wish to slide a trundle bed under this one, just provide for it by building the whole thing one crack higher than otherwise.

With any of these beds, you will need some kind of padding to sleep on. This doesn't have to be a conventional mattress. Folded blankets do fine, as do some of the foam pads sold for backpacking. The pioneers solved the problem by stuffing a cloth sack with whatever dry, soft material was handy —straw, hay, dried-out moss, or even dry leaves. It was changed when it began to mat down and cease to be soft.

TABLES

If you can come by huge log sections, at least 18 inches thick, two of these can be the foundation for a beautiful table. Saw them 27 or 28 inches long. Prepare two slabs the width you want the table, and enough lengthwise slabs to fill that width, and construct a batten door, with pegs or nails, and with the batten slabs recessed at least 18 inches from either end of the table. Then place the completed tabletop with each of the battens directly on top of a log support (in position—you could never move this thing) and put two pegs through into each log. That's all.

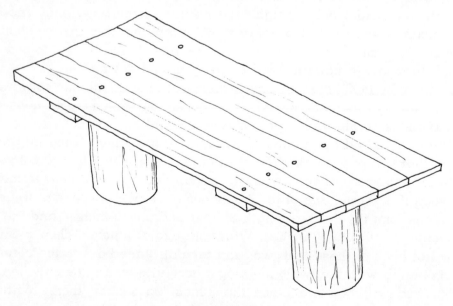

Log-section-supported table.

Table with smaller legs and feet.

If you don't have the huge log sections, you can use a slightly different method. The tabletop is made in the same way as before. For the legs, though, you use two 6-inch logs, from 25 to 27 inches tall, depending on the thickness of your tabletop. The idea is to get the final table height to be about 30 inches. Besides the 6-inch logs, you need two more slabs, each approximately two-thirds the table's width. Attach one slab to the end of each log, pegging through the slab down into the log, two pegs in each. Then stand both legs up, spacing them as you want them for the table, and lay the tabletop on them with each batten directly on top of the leg. Peg the tabletop to the legs with two pegs into each leg, and you're done. If you wish, you can attach braces running horizontally from one leg to the other, but with the table's weight, this shouldn't be necessary.

To make this table without a saw, chop V-notches in the endgrains of the legs-to-be, and use puncheons instead of slabs for the tabletop's battens and for the feet. The V-notches will fit over the puncheons and you can peg through the points, then use corner blocks.

To make a table adjoining the wall, suit the height of the leg to the height of a convenient crack in the wall, attaching the tabletop at the crack, the other end supported by one leg.

If you want a small table, no more than 3 feet square, you can make it with only one leg, with slabs lap-jointed at the bottom to provide you with a pedestal.

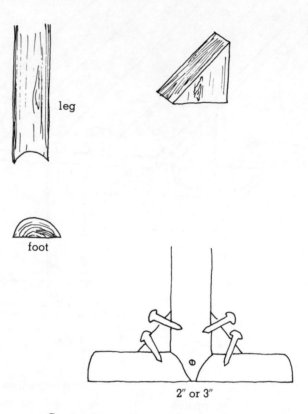

leg

foot

2" or 3"

Construction variations for making
table without a saw.

SHELVES AND PARTITIONS

Given slabs or commercial materials, shelves are easy. If your slabs are
at least 9 inches wide, you can make shelves by laying a slab across two
short upright log sections (sawn ends), then two more log sections, then another slab, and so on. If your slabs aren't that wide, you'll need two of them
per shelf, and consequently a short batten slab pegged or nailed beneath
them at each end to join them securely. The shelves don't have to be pegged
or nailed to the log sections, but it's a good idea to do it.

You can do away with the log-section supports if you want, and substitute
vertical slab supports instead. Just make them either of single slabs, or by
joining together two slabs with battens, in either case making them as tall
as you need. If you've used battens, let them be on the outside rather than
the inside, where they might get in the way of the shelves. Then, all along
the inside at the measured intervals you want, attach more battens, and

when these are done, one shelf can sit across on battens at each end. Attach each shelf permanently, and when done, it will stand. But if it should need extra stability, you can run diagonal braces downwards from the lowest shelf to the floor, and upwards from the top shelf to the wall.

If you have no saw, you'll do better with vertical supports than with log sections. Get the ends of the vertical supports as even as you can, and proceed as above, being sure to run a number of diagonal braces to the wall for stability. If you keep bracing it, sooner or later it will be steady. You can also make the supports out of stone, brick, or block.

You may wonder why we do not mention attaching shelves to a wall, or making pole supports. The reason is this: in a log cabin, either of these ideas is just impossible! You'll make it your life's work to get them anything like even, not to mention parallel. Just make up your mind to build all shelf units basically free-standing. Then if you need to brace it to the wall, fine.

Shelves with log-section supports.

One of the easiest partitions, and a very attractive one, is made of poles used horizontally or vertically. To make them vertical, if you have nails, nail a pole to the ceiling along the line where you want the partition. Attach one just like it to the floor along the same line. Then measure the precise height between, and cut 2-inch poles to that length, making them too long if necessary rather than too short. Chop all the ends off at a slant, then begin nailing them up, top and bottom. Scrunched as close together as possible, they will still leave gaps, and this gives an airy look. If you want complete privacy, use the horizontal system, below, and chink.

If you have no nails, the procedure is slightly different. Peg two poles parallel to the ceiling instead of one, with approximately a 2-inch slot between. Do the same on the floor, if the floor is wood. If you have a dirt or stone floor, construct two small stone walls instead, about 6 inches high and wide, and leave the same 2-inch slot between. With a dirt floor, dig the foot of each pole firmly into the ground. At the end of the wooden or stone slot, block them off, so that the poles won't be able to "walk." Then just fill the space by standing all the poles that will fit in the upper and lower slots.

A horizontal pole partition follows the same theory, but it's turned sideways. You need two pairs of vertical poles running from floor to ceiling with 2-inch gaps between. You can erect these by nailing, or by drilling holes in the floor and ceiling to force the poles if they are green. You can also construct holes for them by surrounding them with blocks of wood, pegged or nailed, or small stones. In a dirt floor you can dig the lower ends in. Once you have them up, all you have to do is keep laying horizontal poles between them all the way up to the top. Chink if desired.

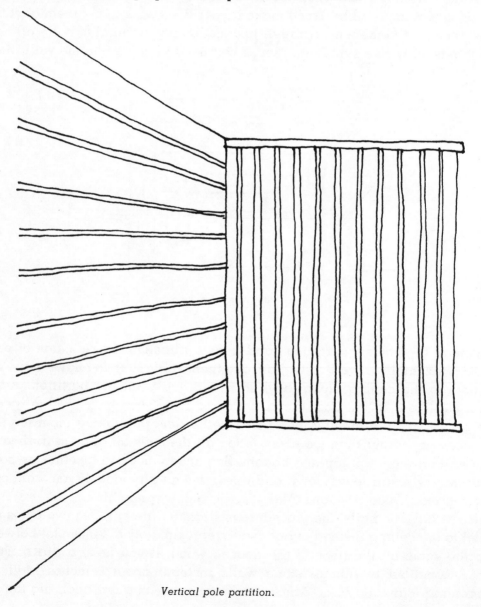

Vertical pole partition.

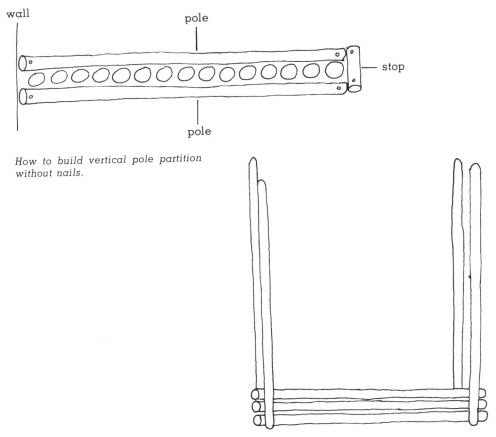

How to build vertical pole partition without nails.

Horizontal pole partition.

To use slabs, follow the same procedures as for poles, whether vertical or horizontal, except that for horizontal use you can just nail or peg them to a single vertical support at each end. Puncheons are not practical for a partition more than 3 feet wide, used horizontally, or 3 feet high, used vertically, due to the difficulty in obtaining them in longer lengths.

Pantries and closets are a combination of partitions and shelves. The best results will be obtained by using slabs for both walls and shelves because of the greater ease in building and more durable product, which more than repays the effort needed to hew them. You can use poles for the walls if you wish, but you'll wish you hadn't when you try to attach shelves to them. In building closets for clothing, if you can use cedar wood or buy cedar particle board, your clothes will keep better from moths.

STAIRS

The simplest of stairs is a ladder. Ladders are completely adequate for climbing up and down, provided you don't have to carry anything. In addition to being easier to build, ladders also take up less space. If you are concerned about carrying things up and down a ladder, you can solve the problem by having a trapdoor in the ceiling, through which you can raise or lower things on a rope. This is easy enough, but if you have a block and tackle you can attach to one of the roof purlins above the trapdoor, it becomes positively effortless. There are several types of ladder you can build easily.

One ladder that the Colonials often used in their never-ending quest to save space and time was a simple series of pegs sticking out of a wall. Such pegs need to be at least 2 inches thick, of a superior pegging wood, and seasoned unless dogwood or hawthorn is used. The entire peg should be about 18 inches long, and 6 inches of that should be sunk into the wall. The finished product is quite strong, picturesque, and efficient.

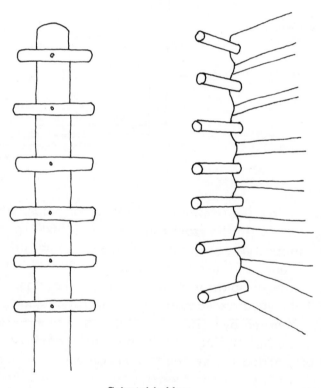

Colonial ladders.

Another type of Colonial ladder is made by using a single substantial post running up to a loft or through the ceiling. The post is notched horizontally every foot to receive crosspieces that are of the same size and characteristics mentioned above, but about 2 feet long. Each is fitted into a notch so that it is flush with the surface of the post, then nailed or pegged in place very securely. This is beautiful, and very strong.

You can easily make a traditional ladder, too, by using the same size rungs, 18 inches long, and attaching them to two verticals 4 or 5 inches thick by the method just discussed.

Stairways of moderate pitch provide more comfort and convenience in the long run, if you have the space. Forty-five degrees is a comfortable angle at which to climb, but even 65 degrees will let you climb without using your hands, once you are used to it. A stairway at a 45-degree pitch will travel forward as far as it goes upward. For example, a 45-degree stair rising 8 feet will also take up 8 feet of floor space. A 65-degree stair rising 8 feet will take up a little less than 5 feet of floor space. So the angle of your stairs depends on the space you've got.

An alternative is to make all or part of your stairway curving. Some of the plans in Chapter 3 were shown using this technique. These can just as well be converted to plain straight ones at a steeper pitch, unless you have technique and time.

Curving stairways are physically easy to build, but the planning and calculating on paper that must come first are maddening, and there is no way for us to include standard instructions for this since it will vary in every case. We have shown one drawing of one, to give the idea. As you can see, one end of each step is notched into a center post, and the other end is supported independently by a vertical slab or a log section. The difficulty is in calculating the heights and angles at which they abut, so that each is spaced exactly like the next and they all exactly fill the space allotted. If you want to sit down and figure all this out for your circumstances, more power to you; but wait until your cabin is built and furnished first, including a simple ladder or straight stair in the meantime.

The space that a straight stairway occupies can be used by putting a window and window seat under it; just raise it high enough that you won't bump your head. You can close in the space for use as a closet, or you can let it rise in the room over a table, bed, or whatever, for a very airy, see-through effect.

To build a plain stairway, begin by marking its position and angle wherever you plan to build it. If it's going to be against a wall, start by marking the floor where it will stand, then measure vertically up the wall to the point where it will enter the upstairs. Draw a slanted line from the very top down to the foot of the stairs, to show the actual incline, and measure along that slanted line to get the length of the slabs you will use in order to support the stairway.

If the stairway will not be along a wall, but free-standing somewhere in the room, mark the floor space it will occupy, as before. Take string and tie it to nails driven into the ceiling and the floor, to construct a string "ghost" of the stairway. Then measure along it, and proceed.

You can use either slabs or puncheons for the steps; puncheons are easier to produce and are stronger and prettier. Their length will depend on what width you want for the stairway. Their length plus the width of the two supports will add up to the stair's total width. A step width of 2 to 2½ feet is fine, and they should be 8 to 10 inches thick, front to back. If you don't have logs that size, use slabs instead, and make each step out of two slabs joined with battens. The two supports should be slabs. On a steep incline, use a 2×6-inch slab, turned on end. On a shallower pitch, use 2×8-inch slabs on end. If you're planning to close in the underneath for use as a closet, and will therefore be using vertical supports as well, you can again decrease the size of the slanted supports a little. But err if necessary on the side of making it overstrong, rather than otherwise.

Now you can assemble the stairway on the ground. Nail or peg the steps to the supports from the outside, through the supports, into the steps. Pegs are much better for this. If nailing, use four or five 20-penny nails in each end. Two half-inch pegs in each end will do. You can space the steps from 9 to 12 inches apart, measured along the support. When you're building this, put only one nail or peg into each end of each step first. Do this with all the steps, then adjust the angle before putting in the rest of the nails or pegs. One way to do this is to set the stairway up in place, angle all the steps so they are level, and put the rest of the nails or pegs in along one support, whichever support you can get to. (If your stairway stands in the middle of the room, you can do both sides and be done with it.) Carefully bring it down again, and do the other side.

Another method of doing this is to measure with a compass or protractor the angle you need, and do it on the ground. A third way is to lay out a triangle on the floor exactly like the one on the wall, and lay your stairway down on its support along the slanted line of it. Then you can position your steps parallel to the base of that triangle and attach them there.

When it's finished, stand it up in its permanent position and attach top and bottom with pegs or nails. At the top, it should be leaning on the edge of the hole it will pass through, and will be easy to attach. But at the bottom, you can use corner blocks to aid in attachment. If it's along a wall, you can also attach it to the wall at one or two additional points if you want.

You may find a banister or rail desirable. If so, it is easy to make. Just attach vertical supports made of poles to a slanting pole rail that is long enough to reach at hand height (about 30 inches) from top to bottom. Do this by notching them together, and then nailing or pegging, or by drilling holes in the rail into which the verticals are fitted with blind wedges. The poles for this should be about 2 inches thick, and there should be three or four of them. Bore holes to fit the verticals into either the stair supports or into the edges of the steps, and fit the verticals into them with blind wedges.

For a banister along the wall, just attach a slanted pole to the wall by means of several blocks nailed or pegged to the wall.

If you intend to completely enclose the area underneath, you will need a door. The easiest way is to make the door the exact width of several of the boards enclosing the space. Decide this before you close it in. Before attaching those particular boards, cut the door out of them, on the ground, and join it with battens. Put an extra crosspiece on the closet, just above the door's height, to attach the pieces of board left after cutting out the door. Then fit the door into its space, and hinge it. This is much easier than enclosing the whole space, and trying to cut the door out afterwards.

Having gotten this far, nothing is left but the frosting on the cake. Such things as pegs on the back of doors, lamp brackets, and curtains will suggest themselves. It is also sometimes desirable to paint ceilings white between beams to amplify light. And there are rugs, and handmade rush mats, and colorful cushions. All these ornamental touches can make an unbelievable difference in the looks of a cabin. Other touches, too, will suggest themselves as you live there longer and your cabin begins to reflect you and your distinctive taste. But that's what the cabin is all about—providing a stable and congenial platform for your existence, so that you can confidently embark on the rest of your life.

Bon voyage!

INDEX